A World Unsuspected

A World Unsuspected

A Red Wheelbarrow Writers Anthology

Sidekick Press
Bellingham, Washington

Published 2025
Printed in the United States of America
ISBN 978-1-958808-40-5

Sidekick Press
2950 Newmarket Street
Suite 101–329
Bellingham, WA 98226
sidekickpress.com

Cover Design: Andrea Gabriel

CONTENTS

so much depends
upon

a red wheel
barrow

glazed with rain
water

beside the white
chickens.

William Carlos Williams
XXII from *Spring and All* (1923)

Introduction

Red Wheelbarrow Writers is a loose affiliation of writers who join together to support, encourage, and sustain one another. We have no dues or formal order of responsibility. When we need money, we pass the hat. When we have an important endeavor, we show up. We welcome all writers, whether novice or experienced, to our monthly Happy Hour to drink wine, share excerpts of works-in-progress, and exchange news and views. We sometimes meet for write-outs, a day spent writing together in unique settings. Red Wheelbarrow Writers participates in the annual April National Poetry Month with a dedicated Facebook page. In November, National Novel Writing Month, we collectively write a novel, with chaotic and often hilarious results.

We also publish anthologies. *A World Unsuspected* is our fifth. The title comes from "The Descent," a poem by Williams Carlos Williams, whose poetry gave Red Wheelbarrow Writers its name. In our call for submissions, we asked for fiction, nonfiction, and poetry that captures the importance of a particular place and its power to surprise, transform, and inspire. Williams' keen observation of everyday scenes reveals how simple, seemingly mundane encounters can have a profound impact. We sought pieces that explore how the experience of a place can alter perspective, shift understanding, or spark a revelation.

The unique voices assembled in this volume will take you on a journey to places as varied as the wilds of Alaska, the heat of North Africa, a family farm in Tennessee, the green hills of Devon, and back again to the beloved mountains and islands of the Pacific Northwest. You will travel in time as well—back to childhood memories and the adventures of college days, at times even venturing into a magical dimension. We hope this collection of poetry and prose takes you on a voyage of discovery that does indeed surprise and inspire you.

Hats Off
by Bob Warren

Milton wore his drab green felt fedora like a football helmet, tight over his ears and forehead. He could see his shoes better than the sky. Like Milton himself, the hat was frayed, stained, a bit sullen, and worn with years.

Milton walked to his job at the bank each day. He would pass the same familiar homes on the same familiar streets. He would visit the same bakery for his usual cup of mediocre coffee, then continue along the boulevard on the ridge of the hill. The maple tree roots had heaved up the sidewalks, slowing his way, but from there, he could gaze out over the endless ocean and dream.

The bank where he worked was impressive—strong and stoic. It resembled a fortress, with its tall, featureless walls buttressed by squat-clipped hedges and thick stone pillars standing at attention. Milton had worked there for what seemed his whole life. His desk in the basement had never moved. Alone all day, he would sit and count things—assets and debits, gains and losses—doing whatever he was told. He had asked once to work upstairs, somewhere with people, and maybe near a window. But no, they told him, he worked best alone, and a window would only distract him.

Often, his walk home was the best part of his day. One evening, though, there was a problem. The city was repairing the sidewalks along the boulevard. Jackhammers had already destroyed the cement, and bright yellow WARNING tape surrounded the area. He surveyed the site for a path through the debris, but his way was blocked. With a sigh, he resigned himself to finding a different way home. Soon, he was lost among unfamiliar shops on unfamiliar streets. He passed a cluttered antique shop, a curious-looking bookstore, and a small café, but all were closed except the Crown Haberdashery.

The haberdashery was an older building of brick and mortar, at one time grand and ornate but now faded and pitted by years of weather. It looked out of place among the newer and simpler buildings nearby. In the shop's front window, handsome mannequins stood dressed in tailored suits, with silk neckties and gleaming polished shoes. Milton's reflection in the same glass window revealed his department-store shirt, his discount-rack slacks, and, of course, his old fedora. A sign on the door said: WELCOME: PLEASE COME IN!

Curious, Milton pulled open the heavy wooden door. The shop smelled of cedar, a hint of cologne, and something like an unfamiliar spice. A crystal chandelier dimly lit the plaster ceiling cast with interlaced vines. Dark wood paneled walls surrounded the room, protecting it from the outside world. At his feet, a finely woven rug led further into the room, like a welcoming path. Milton hesitated but then removed his hat and tentatively entered. The lights brightened, revealing more of the room. It was silent. Was he alone?

Along the central aisle, orderly rows of beautiful jackets, slacks, and suits greeted him. Silk neckties of every color and pattern hung on a wall like trophies or awards. Polished, mahogany cabinets promised even more. In the center of the room, he found six gilded glass cases set side by side like in a museum. Slowly, he stepped from one case to another, examining a trove of finery: beautiful gold watches, jeweled cufflinks, silver money clips, and more. Dazzled, Milton hardly breathed. He had never seen such opulence before.

The chandeliers overhead flickered once. The wooden door behind him closed without a sound.

"How may I assist you?" said a resonant voice.

Startled, Milton turned with a gasp, dropping his hat. A man now stood there, tall and dark, wearing an elegant suit. How had he appeared?

Milton stiffened and cleared his throat. "I'm sorry," he mumbled, reaching down for his hat. "I didn't see you."

"Of course," said the man with a slight polite bow. "Welcome, I am Gazi. How may I help you?" His voice was gracious and pleasing, and he seemed somehow ageless with his thick grey hair and his face uncreased and unweathered.

Milton stepped away, back toward the door. "I'm sorry. I'm lost."

"Not likely, Sir," Gazi replied. "What are you seeking?"

"I guess I don't really know," he admitted with a sigh.

"Perhaps a new hat?" Gazi said pleasantly with a slight nod to Milton's old fedora.

"Well . . ." Milton said, glancing around the room. Everything looked so expensive. "I probably can't afford anything here."

"Perhaps what you need is priceless. Follow me this way, if you would." He gestured for Milton to follow.

The backroom was splendid, decorated with hats of every sort, displayed on the walls like ornaments. A warm light from an unseen source filled the room with an ethereal glow. Milton stood speechless, amazed.

"What is it you seek, Sir? What do you need?"

Milton shrugged. He'd never seen so many hats, of every sort and color! How could he possibly choose?

"If I may suggest, Sir," Gazi said, "something bold and strong, perhaps? Something proud and confident, like a fresh, new you?" Bewildered, Milton bit his lip but nodded.

"Clothes do make the man, after all," Gazi stated with some authority. "I believe I may have just what you need."

Gazi stepped away but soon returned. "This should be the one, Sir. It seems made just for you."

Milton watched intently as Gazi set the hatbox on the counter, lifted its lid, and carefully removed the hat. He offered it to Milton like a precious gift—a handsome brown suede trilby, shapely and distinct, banded with a black silk ribbon.

Cautiously, as though afraid to touch it, Milton accepted the hat and delicately set it on his head. He turned to the mirror and considered his image. He adjusted it carefully from side to side until it was perfect. It fit him like a crown. He beamed with pride at his reflection. He looked like a new man.

In the morning, Milton wore his new hat to work, eager to impress everyone. His colleagues all greeted him by name. The pretty secretary gave him a smile. Even his boss was impressed: "Milton, my friend, your work is important. You deserve a desk by the window."

When Milton returned home after work that day, his neighbor, Mrs. Schneider, called to him from her front porch. "Good evening, Milton. You are looking well." Surprised, he replied with a wave. They had hardly ever spoken before.

The next day, wearing his splendid new hat, he walked to work a different way. He discovered a pretty flower shop, a colorful fruit stand, and a café with good coffee. He arrived at work early and eager to work. The time passed quickly, and he accomplished more than ever. When Milton looked up from his desk, he would gaze at the view from his window, across the endless ocean.

That evening, Mrs. Schneider greeted him again. "You are looking well, Milton."

He replied with a smile. "Yes, good evening, Ma'am. I hope you've had a nice day."

These daily greetings soon became their evening routine. Then they would sit together watching the sunset and reflecting on the busy day—things that had happened, things that had not, and what might happen next.

Walking to work along the boulevard one Monday morning, the pavement now smooth and the sidewalk repaired, Milton gazed out over the ocean. Its tossing waves glistened. Sleek sailboats raced across the water. Seagulls floated like kites in the breeze. Milton raised his face to the bright, warm sun and closed his eyes with a satisfied sigh. But just then, like a playful child, a brisk breeze swept past, and away flew his hat!

"No!" he cried out, leaping and lunging for it. But he could only watch as it sailed away. It settled onto the rocks far below and soon drowned in the waves, gone. Breathless, he moaned, staring down at the rocks. What could he do?

Abruptly, the sunny sky grew cloudy, and the day turned cold. But Milton lingered, despondent. Rain began to fall. Hatless, he plodded his way to work. He passed the same old houses on the same old streets. He passed the old bakery with its mediocre coffee. He continued along the boulevard, but all he could see was grey. The rain became a storm.

At work, he arrived wet and cold. No one noticed he was late. At his desk, he found a plain cardboard box. Scowling, he looked around, but no one would meet his gaze. What was wrong? What had happened?

In the box were his pencils, papers, and other things, and a handwritten note: "There has been a mistake. This desk is not yours. Yours is in the basement where you left it." No one had bothered to sign it. His eyes welled with tears. His face grew red and hot. He turned away, leaving the cardboard box on the desk. Furious, he stormed from the office—finished with his time at the bank.

Standing still on the sidewalk outside, he watched, without seeing, the rain fall and puddle in the street. Soon, his face was as wet as his coat, but he did not notice or care. A stranger brushed past him on the sidewalk, stirring Milton from his thoughts. He stared, sullen, as the stranger walked away, wearing a beautiful hat.

Milton gasped. He began to trot and then to run. He ran past the antique shop, the curious bookstore, and the café with good coffee. He didn't stop until finally he stood, breathless and spent, in front of the Crown Haberdashery.

A sign on the door read: WELCOME: PLEASE COME IN! The room welcomed him, warm and quiet. His wet shoes made hardly a sound as he stepped across the woven wool rug. The dim chandelier overhead flickered once.

"How may I assist you, Sir?" said a resonant voice.

Milton turned, and there stood Gazi in his elegant suit. Milton cleared his throat. "It's not my fault, but I've lost my hat. I need another just like it," he pleaded.

Looking thoughtful, Gazi considered Milton—his posture, his bearing, especially his eyes. He then nodded. "Follow me this way, if you would."

The hat room was still splendid, but not like before. Different hats now hung on the walls—different shapes and colors, no two alike. The light in the room was now crisp and bright. The air smelled clean and fresh.

"I believe I may have just what you need," Gazi said kindly, and he stepped away. Soon he returned with a fine hatbox. "This should be the one, Sir. It seems made just for you."

Milton watched intently as Gazi set the hatbox on the counter, lifted its lid, and carefully removed the hat. He offered it to Milton like a precious gift—a drab green felt fedora, frayed, stained, and familiar.

Perplexed, Milton scowled and furrowed his brow. "No, that's not right. That's not the one. I can't be like that again."

Gazi did not reply.

"Like you said, clothes make the man. But I'm not like that anymore. I need a new hat," Milton begged.

"Yes," Gazi said, his voice kind and patient, "a man's clothes may shape his image, how others perceive him, but a man's choices are always his own." He offered the fedora to Milton again. "This one seems made just for you."

Milton accepted it, though dubiously. He gently turned it from hand to hand. The smooth felt was soft with age, and its bent brim frayed and worn. Yet it felt familiar, like an old friend.

He set it on his head and turned to the mirror. In his reflection, he saw a man who looked dashing in a vintage fedora—a man who deserved a fulfilling job and a good cup of coffee. A man worthy of respect.

He turned to Gazi. "It's perfect," he beamed. "It fits me like a crown."

That evening, he and Mrs. Schneider sat together watching the sun set and reflecting on the day. "I quit my job," he said with a satisfied sigh. "I'm ready for a change."

She touched his hand. "You deserve to be happy, Milton."

He drew a deep breath. "Would you have breakfast with me tomorrow? I know a café with good coffee."

Consecrated Ground
by Tyson Higel

Ordination in the ordinary—
This space, where we wash dishes
and do laundry, is a testament
to all the Love and Thoughtfulness we choose.

I've chosen these chores today,
on my day off, while you're away
at work, not purely out of necessity,
but because I've chosen you.

A clean home is a sacrament.
It's not an obligation, it's
something I want to do. I want
to ease your mind,

and make Peace, here, in our home.
It's directly correlated—
this structure of steel and plaster,
your structure of veins and bones.

Present in each, the Divine.
Sacred acts of Love that reach
through time, that manifest
in folded laundry, clean dishes, kisses.

Mrs. Crump, Alcoves, and Dark, Silent Areas: More Necessary Than Ever
by Linda Lambert

Susan Orleans's *The Library Book* chronicles the 1986 fire at the Los Angeles Public Library. The conflagration reached 2,000 degrees, burned for seven hours, and incinerated 400,000 books. Raising the millions of dollars to replace the building and the collection took six years, demonstrating Angelenos' support for their public library.

My book club's discussion of Orleans' book generated a flurry of personal remembrances so interesting that I asked members to put pens to paper and fingers to keyboards. Their stories—edited, excerpted, and paraphrased with their permission—convey the importance and relevance of libraries everywhere.

Elsie Heinrick recalls Mr. Cockburn, the librarian, when she was a ninth grader at Mission BC High School.

> He was "amenable and helpful, but also strange in many ways . . . quite quirky." After enthusing that she'd love to

be a librarian, he paused and said, "Elsie, don't you know that women librarians have the lowest marriage rates?"

Kay Ingram recalled the first time she opened the doors of a white, Colonial-style building on Main Street in Plymouth, Michigan, in the mid-1940s:

> I entered a dark, silent area crowded with shelves. Not at all inviting, no smiles offered by anyone. I did read books as a child, but I went to the library not because I was drawn to stories or adventures or opportunities for discovery. I went to the library to find and read what was assigned. I *had* to go. However, that early library experience did not stop me from being an avid reader as an adult. Reading *The Library Book* took me on a journey of discovery and enlightenment.

Jayne Freudenberger did not have access to a neighborhood library. She did have access to the school library at Girls' Preparatory School in Chattanooga, Tennessee. GPS was for rich kids. Jayne, a scholarship student, was not one of them. "In the South, GPS was the girls' equivalent to boys' military schools and the only place to get a good education. The city's schools were deplorable." As a seventh grader, Jayne delighted in GPS's large library with friends who shared her love of books.

> My classmate Catherine and I formed a sort of friendly rivalry to see how fast we could get through the junior section of books (for seventh and eighth grades). I have no recollection of the book titles. We read them quickly. One day, we picked out a few from the senior section and took them to the librarian to check out. She sternly reproved us

for "shopping" in the wrong section and had no sympathy when we told her we had read everything in the junior section. That only reinforced our desire to read the "forbidden books."

Jayne and Catherine petitioned the principal, who called them into her office.

Mrs. Tucker had iron-gray hair; *iron* was the right word for the rest of her, too. There were no smiles as we walked in the door. "Catherine and Jayne," she said, "I hear you have a complaint." Catherine cringed; Jayne spoke softly. "Well, not a complaint, more like a request."

Mrs. Tucker said she understood that they'd read all the seventh and eighth grade books and asked if they had also read the encyclopedias cover-to-cover. They admitted they had read some volumes, but not all, and not cover-to-cover.

Mrs. Tucker smiled. "Well, I guess that's all right. Neither have I." She gave a little laugh. "Far be it that I would refuse to let any of my girls read. Here, I have stamped your cards with senior privileges . . . come back and tell me how you liked the senior library."

Jayne and Catherine practically bowed their way out of the office, murmuring, "Thank you, thank you." Jayne still remembers one of the books she checked out, *Dinner at Antoine's* by Frances Parkinson Keys.

Years later, like many book lovers who hope to pass their enthusiasm on to children and grandchildren, Jayne remembers taking her three-year-old granddaughter Ana to the Children's Room.

When we walked in, her face broke into a wide smile. She kept turning around, taking in all of the shelves. When she learned she could take books home, she almost cleared those shelves. Now twenty-eight, Ana reads constantly. We exchange book titles whenever we are together, but I haven't recommended *Dinner at Antoine's*. Yet.

Jayme Curley recalled her growing-up years on an island in Puget Sound in the 1940s and '50s. Though the island had no library, each of the six classrooms in her grade school contained a small bookshelf "stocked with wonderful books." She and her friend Judy Loken raced each other to get first pick of the horse books.

Our world expanded with the arrival of a bookmobile, a friendly, airless place with a sympathetic librarian—and stuffed with horse books. We were allowed to check out three per visit. Heaven!

Heaven didn't last long. The bookmobile was discontinued, and "there ensued this long library blankness. One summer, as a bored teenager, I devoured our family's set of *Great Books* in one long swallow."

After attending a boarding school for girls, Jayme went to Wellesley. "I took every possible literature class. I read what was assigned without realizing there was no rule against free grazing beyond assignments. Eventually, I discovered bookstores. I now treat Village Books as my library."

Growing up in Edina, Minnesota, **Betsy Gross** loved the library: "a converted white clapboard house located on a hill . . . the front and side yards were shaded by multiple pine trees, adding to its appearance as a welcoming country home."

Betsy recalled that the librarian, Mrs. Crump, "was an old lady—from my youthful perspective. She was willowy thin, had a hooked nose, and smelled of talcum powder. She always wore dresses with pressed collars, glasses hanging on a chain around her neck."

In winter, Betsy spent most Saturdays at the library at a special reading place: an alcove whose window looked out on the side yard's trees.

> I can still see it. Mrs. Crump took a special interest in me, helping me find books I'd like. I thought of her as my friend. She honored my interest in horses, introducing me to every book about horses in the library. Some Saturdays, I would find one left for me in the alcove. She is why I read *Old Yeller, My Friend Flicka, Anne of Green Gables, The Wind in the Willows, Black Beauty,* and the C.S. Lewis series.

Sometimes, Betsy, arriving late, would find the alcove occupied by . . .

> someone whom I believed did not belong there! I took a seat at what I felt was a cold, unwelcoming table, keeping one eye on the interloper until they left so I could regain my rightful place. Mrs. Crump apparently noticed this behavior. One Saturday morning, I arrived a little late and found Mrs. Crump sitting in the alcove, holding my seat for me. With a smile and a new book for my consideration, she politely reminded me to arrive when the library opened.

The Edina Library carried Betsy through her childhood Saturdays, giving her "refuge away from the chaos of my home life and opening me to a world of new ideas, experiences, and ways to live. Mrs. Crump gave me two precious gifts that I still keep in my pocket: a love of books and spending leisurely days getting lost in them, and to never underestimate the kindness of strangers."

Pam Sankey, her husband, and her daughter, Jessica, were in New Zealand on an extended visit with Pam's sister. When Jessica heard New Zealand children started kindergarten on their fifth birthday, she became curious about the one-room schoolhouse up the hill.

Jessica insisted she would like to spend her birthday visiting the school. We packed her a snack, let her dress in a going-to-visit-school outfit, and walked her to school, expecting that would be the end of school. Jessica had other ideas. At day's end, she bounced out of the schoolroom with a bag of *Red Readers*, ready-to-read texts provided to all New Zealand primary school children. She had a homework sheet for everyone in the household to sign, confirming she had read to each of us. Jessica attended school every day while we went about our planned adventures. She had decided to officially become a reader.

Years later, as a middle schooler, Jessica frequented the Hollywood Neighborhood Library in Portland, Oregon. She claimed she needed to finish her homework at the library for the next day.

We later discovered that she liked the library's quiet, comfortable space for reading. Starting on the JF shelf, she read her way through it, the YF shelf, and beyond. When it was time to leave her favorite chair, she bookmarked her place and tucked the book under the chair's cushion so it would be ready for her the next day.

The first library **Jane Volland** remembers was in a large home at the corner of Evans and Genesee streets in Auburn, New York, two blocks away from home.

I remember being happy when I was old enough to go alone without my mother or little sister. Finding a book seemed like a serious adventure, along with receiving a yellow card stamped and initialed by the librarian, Mrs. Shelton, who added a strict verbal warning about the due date. I read all the *Five Little Peppers* volumes, Nancy Drew mysteries, and, later, the romance novels of Frank Yerby. I don't think I showed the latter to my parents.

In Jane's high school library, she checked out books about girls who became ballerinas, stewardesses, successful detectives, and women who rode in championship horse races. Later, after reading a Eugene O'Neill play, she went to the Case Memorial Library, "a beautiful 1896 building in downtown Auburn," to read more of O'Neill.

I discovered not only the O'Neill plays but the joy of sitting in the private quiet of a magnificent setting. I sat at a large, carved wooden table in a small, ornate room with floor-to-ceiling bookshelves; usually, I was the only person there.

That experience may have been the reason she was drawn to little rooms in large libraries.

As a student at Middlebury College in Vermont, I studied in the small, book-filled Robert Frost room. As a graduate student at New York University, I enjoyed exploring the stacks and discovering books I didn't know existed. Studying at the big New York Public Library on Fifth Avenue and walking past the lions to find a spot in the impressive reading room was a special treat!

In the late 1960s, Jane was teaching criminology in the sociology department at San Francisco State. Researching in a law library was the catalyst for changing her career:

> I realized that the legal perspective attracted me more than the sociological one I had pursued. Many years later, after marriage and two children, I began law school as the oldest person in my class at Duke Law School. I attended early morning classes and spent time with study, research, and writing in the Duke Law Library while my husband took care of things at home. Later, I utilized the University of North Carolina's Law Library near our home in Chapel Hill.

She also enjoyed taking her children and grandchildren to libraries for books or storytelling. "Libraries," she enthuses, "have provided me a lifetime of joy."

Amory Peck grew up hearing, "I *need* to go to the library." She can't remember a time when her grandmother, mother, and father were without a library book at hand. Her grandmother obtained books from the main branch of the Detroit Library, which was . . .

> a grand facility, with broad, long stairs leading up from the entry to the library itself. In the middle of those stairs stood a large, bronze lion, his nose rubbed shiny from the pats received from every person climbing. I was encouraged to

pat the lion. At other places, I was told, "Keep your hands to yourself. Don't touch."

Amory's hometown library in St. Clair, Michigan, was simpler. It was located on the bottom floor of a creaky old building smelled of varnish, dust, and books.

As a child, I had to walk through the adult section, past the librarian's desk, and down a hallway to the children's room with low shelves, small tables and chairs, and lots of books to take home. From an early age, I was a reader, too. In the best sense of the word, going to the library was ordinary. Mama might say, "I have to pick up some bread and tomatoes, then I'll go and get some books." Daddy might say, "I'll swing by the hardware store, then go to the library." Library books were always in our house. I grew up assuming that libraries were part of life as usual. Not extraordinary, just essential.

As I, **Linda**, read through the recollections of my book club friends, I found them similar to those of my growing-up years. Though my childhood was stable and uncomplicated, a Mrs. Crump existed in my library life: Goldie Stewart at the Visalia Public Library in California. One day, as I waited for the *thunk-clack-snap* of the date stamp on the inside covers of my books, she said, with a happy smile, "I walked by your house, and I heard you singing from your bedroom window." I don't know how the startled ten-year-old me responded. I do know that Mrs. Stewart was the first librarian to demonstrate personal interest in me. When, in later life, I became a librarian and a library director, Goldie Stewart was the first of many librarian role models.

Now that I am retired, I still go to libraries. One day, wandering through the Ferndale branch of the Whatcom County Library System, I strolled by dozens of colorful paperbacks displayed for "tweens" (a category that didn't exist when I was a tween). I saw a diversity of patrons, including two badge-wearing missionaries working at the computers, six teenagers perched on low cabinets of a meeting room, and moms with children gathering for story time. Posters dotted an entrance wall advertising myriad WCLS opportunities, activities, and publications: tech help, an art and audiobook listening activity, teen gaming, Lego Club, art exhibits, *Whatcomics*, and Whatcom Reads.

Libraries continue to define and redefine themselves, adapting to the needs of the communities they serve. They rest comfortably in the category of "Third Places," a term created by sociologist Roy Oldenberg in *The Great Good Place* (1989) to describe areas where people gather, away from their first and second places: home and work.

However similar or dissimilar the memories of twenty-first-century library-goers are to those of our earlier generation, I concur with the reviewer who calls Susan Orlean's *The Library Book* "a master journalist's reminder that, perhaps, especially in the digital era, [libraries] are more necessary than ever."

Artwork
by Michelle DiSarno

We made universes in the stone yard, that wonderland
boxed by the white picket fence, that place

where we lived while you cleaned our dinner
over a bucket. I can still hear the snapping

of the crabs' underbellies, as I can feel the smooth
stones cupped in my palm. Our pockets held them

in bulges; at dusk, we skipped them across
the rocks, looking for a spark of light,

a firecracker tiny enough for our world.
When it rained, and the ocean turned

gray with a milk mustache, and the pale browns
of the stones darkened with wetness, we lived

our waiting behind streaky windows
amid sketch pads and crayons. And as if

you could put a price on the pure act
of creation, we signed each picture and tagged

"25 cents" on the back. It was a business, our way
of pocketing snow-cone and skee-ball money.

We showcased the drawings like we were selling
life insurance, always somehow interrupting dinner.

But I went straight to you. You put down your fork,
wiped the butter from your hands, and gave

the drawing a long look, like I knew you would.
I'd like to buy this one, you said with conviction.

It's hard to remember if my five-year-old mind
suspected that it was all a game we played,

that the stick figures and scratchy coloring
were no good and you were just being polite.

But what did it matter? Because when you handed me
a whole dollar bill and said, "Keep the change,"

I was Picasso; I may as well have been a millionaire.

The Springhouse
by John Miller

Each summer, my older sisters, Miriam and Patsy, and I spent two weeks of our summer vacation with Nanny and Grandpa Langer at their farmhouse on the western edge of Paxanosa, Pennsylvania. Most family farms had been parceled and sold off before the War. All that remained was an old farmhouse made of fieldstone, a summer kitchen, and a springhouse. We didn't realize it then, but those summer visits were some of the happiest days we would ever spend.

One day in mid-July of 1959, I was sitting at the kitchen table trying to decipher some German words written under the distelfinks, those stylized images of birds that the Pennsylvania Dutch love. They covered the tablecloth Nanny had just stretched across her long kitchen table. She'd been talking, but I hadn't been listening. Then she said something that caught my interest.

". . . and of course, Jimmy, that was before we had the power."

"Power?" I asked, perking up immediately. I imagined some godlike force entering the family homestead from an alien planet.

"Yes, but we didn't get the power until just before the Great War."

"The Civil War?" I asked.

"No! World War One!" She laughed. "We didn't get electricity until then."

"Oh."

I was disappointed. I had hoped it was more than electricity powering that ancient farmhouse and the land itself. I would soon learn that there was indeed a magic in the land, but not the kind you read about in *The Brothers Grimm*. This was real magic, yet magic so familiar I didn't even know it was there until I felt the pee running down my pant leg.

It started that afternoon. My sisters and I went outside before dinner to play hide and seek. Whenever we stayed at Nanny and Grandpa's, we played hide and seek almost every day, but until that summer afternoon in 1959, I had never won. No matter where I hid—under my grandparents' bed, behind the old wringer washing machine in the cellar, or even in the hall closet—Miriam and Patsy always found me. On that July afternoon, it seemed this game would end like all the others.

Patsy had lost at "odds and evens," and she was "it." As always, she wasted no time arguing that Miriam and I had cheated. But she soon gave up, and with a shrug, she walked over to the old apple tree in the backyard, turned her back to us, leaned against the tree trunk, and began counting down from a hundred.

Miriam ran to find a hiding place, but I sat down on the grass next to the flagstone path to think while Patsy droned out the numbers. With my eyes closed, I mulled over all the good places I could hide. But Patsy knew me too well. She'd find me, unless . . . unless I could find a place where she'd never bother to look. I took a deep breath. I hadn't a clue. Darn! I was going to lose again. I'd already tried every hiding place on the farm—inside and outside the house—except . . . except . . . I exhaled slowly, opened my eyes, and saw the low gable and slate roof of the stone springhouse, not too far from where I sat. Then, inspiration. That's it! I'll hide in the springhouse!

I had visited the springhouse only a few times and always with Grandpa or my dad. I had never thought of hiding there. None of us had. It was a scary place, a low stone edifice with a slate roof rising painfully out of the earth like the gateway to the River Styx. The front wall was made of fieldstone, but the rest was carved out of the living limestone.

I dashed down the flagstone pavement to the springhouse. Little pools of water splashed under my feet as I skidded down the six stone steps to the heavy wooden doorway that was half-buried underground. I reached out a hand; the wood was slimy to the touch as if an army of slugs had crawled over it. Overcoming my revulsion, I grasped the handle. It had rained hard the night before. I suppose that was why I had such a difficult time getting the door open. I pulled on it twice but moved it only an inch or two, its bottom scraping heavily against the slate threshold. Patsy's voice droned on. "Thirty-one, thirty, twenty-nine . . ."

I had to get in there fast. I gave the door one mighty tug. It made a loud screech and opened a little. A musty scent rushed out to envelop me, as if the place had widened its dark maw and breathed on me. The gap was just wide enough for my slim nine-year-old body to slip in. Inside, it smelled like animals long dead. The air was cool and clammy. But I was not ready to relax just yet. Patsy was nearing the end. I could barely hear her now.

"Fifteen, fourteen, thirteen . . ."

Turning around in the dim light, I grasped the old doorknob on the inside. With all my strength, I gave it a titanic yank and pulled the door shut. Its bottom made a loud rasp that echoed inside. I felt some pride at my efforts until I realized how dank and dark it was now. Every time I'd visited before, Grandpa had left the door open. There was no electricity and no light except the feeble rays that seeped in through the cracks above the door and under the eaves of the slate roof.

A ledge of slate led from the doorway to the edge of the spring. The ledge was just wide enough for me to lie down on. And that's what I did, propping my head against the wall next to the door. When I stretched out my legs, my feet came to rest on the very edge of the spring.

I shivered as I lay in the darkness, feeling the cold, damp slate against my back and legs. And then I began to hear things. There was a constant gurgling, like an elf trying to clear its throat, and a low howling sound seeping through crevices in the wall. The howling seemed to grow louder, and a thought crept into my mind, sending another shiver down my spine. *This springhouse . . . this damned place is alive,* I thought.

Maybe it was not a springhouse at all, but a living tomb. And the tomb was howling.

I'm getting the hell out of here, I thought, then chastised myself. *Why, oh why, did I have to use the word "damned," and now "hell," in this hellish place?* I jumped up and pushed hard on the door, but it wouldn't budge. I pushed with every ounce of strength, every sinew in my body. Nothing.

Outside, Patsy shouted, "Olly, olly, oxen free!"

I had won. But I didn't care. I just wanted to get out of there. I heard Patsy shout the all-clear signal several times more; I still couldn't get the door open. I continued shoving on the door and shouting in a frenzied voice as loud as I could, "I'm here! I'm here! I'm here!"

I heard Miriam and Patsy yelling, "Jimmy! Jimmy!"

Soon, Nanny and Grandpa's voices joined the chorus. I shouted back, still pushing on the door, but no luck. I gave the door one more mighty shove. Nothing. It was then I felt a warm stream of urine running down the left pantleg of my jeans and into my Converse high tops. I threw myself onto the slate ledge and began to weep. *I'm going to die here*, I thought, and started laughing hysterically. Soon, I was totally exhausted and fell into a deep slumber, the voices of loved ones calling ever more faintly in my ears.

And then I began to dream. So utterly vivid was the dream that I remember all of it to this day. The funny thing is that I rarely recall anything when I wake, but every dream that I do remember has one aspect in common: my cousin Reenie is in it. As I faded into dreamland, I found myself standing outside the parsonage of St. Paul's Lutheran Church on Maple Street, looking up at my cousin Reenie Schaffer. She was gazing down at me from her bedroom window and singing.

Reenie was six years older than me, the daughter of my father's elder sister Alice and her husband, Reverend Hal Schaffer, Paxanosa's Lutheran minister. Reenie'd had a hard road to travel since the very moment of her birth. It had been a difficult delivery, and old Doc Nussbaum had had to pull her out by the head with forceps. He had squeezed too hard, and there was brain damage. He had also managed somehow to twist Reenie's spine radically and irrevocably to the left. Perhaps Doc was losing his touch, or maybe what he saw gave him such a shock that he tightened his grip and twisted the forceps. After delivering hundreds of Paxanosa's babies, Doc Nussbaum saw for the first time an infant with a caul covering not only her face but her entire head. The whole delivery had shaken old Doc up, according to Nanny, who had been in the room when Reenie was born. The hard squeeze to Reenie's cranium left her able to read and write, but just barely. Her back never straightened despite the use of braces and countless treatments. By 1959, when Reenie was just sixteen, Uncle Hal and Aunt Alice had given up taking her to specialists. The unkind circumstances of her birth had sentenced her to walk as though she were bending her left ear to the ground and listening. Perhaps it was meant to be. She heard things that others could not.

Despite all this, Reenie was in possession of the sunniest disposition in Paxanosa. Her real name was Eileen Ann Schaffer, but everyone called her Reenie because that was what she called herself. Reenie had a problem pronouncing words. She always called me "Deemie." She just couldn't get her tongue around the "J" or the "I" sound in the name "Jimmy" or the "L" sound in "Eileen." In truth, she had an odd way of saying everyone's name.

But there I was, in a dream, standing in front of the parsonage and looking up at Reenie as she sang. It was daytime, but the light was an unearthly shade of amber, like Neuweiler beer. Reenie stopped singing.

"Hi, Deemie."

"Hi, Reenie. Whatcha singing?"

"'Over the Rainbow.' Do you know it, Deemie?" Reenie had two favorite songs, "Jesus Loves Me" and "Over the Rainbow." She sang them every chance she got.

"Yes, I do, Reenie."

"Sing it with me, Deemie."

And we began to sing, "Somewhere over the rainbow, way up high. There's a land that I heard of once in a lullaby."

"Sing louder, Deemie! Aunt Mitchie can't hear you!"

Aunt Mitchie was my mother. Her real name was Mitzi, but "Mitchie" was what Reenie always called her.

"Okay," I said. "I will if you will." I sang loud. As loud as I could. We both did.

And we kept on singing until, still in my dream, I heard faint voices shouting somewhere in the distance. They came closer. One sounded like Mom, the other like Grandpa.

"Jimmy!" shouted Grandpa, sounding far away.

Mom, too, was off in the distance, calling me.

"Where's my little boy?" she shouted, her voice cracking. "Where's my Jimmy?"

Still asleep, and still singing in my dream, I looked up and noticed that the parsonage, along with Reenie in the window, was drifting away in a bank of swirling clouds. Then I heard someone pounding heavily on wood and a loud scraping sound as the door to the springhouse grated open. Suddenly, Mom was kneeling beside me, hugging me and covering my face with kisses. She was crying.

"Mom! Stop! I'm okay," I said.

I saw Grandpa standing in the doorway, smiling and holding a flashlight. I smelled the cool night air blowing in from outside and saw stars twinkling through the doorway. It was nighttime.

"Wait 'til your father hears about this!" Mom said, still hugging me so tightly I could hardly breathe. Dad wasn't there. He'd been working the middle shift at Bethlehem Steel all week and wouldn't be home 'til after midnight. Then Mom began turning her head this way and that as though she were looking for something—or someone.

"Where is she, Grandpa? She's not here! What happened to her?"

"Where's who?" I asked.

"Why, Reenie, of course. We heard the two of you singing 'Somewhere over the Rainbow' at the top of your lungs. How did she get out of here?"

"She's not here, Mom," I said. "I mean, she wasn't here at all. She's at home. She's singing from the window of her room."

"I guess we were hearing things, Mitzi," said Grandpa, nodding at me, a knowing look in his eyes.

"We were not hearing things," said Mom, a fierce tone entering her voice that I had never heard before. Then she paused and stared at Grandpa for a long moment and gave me another hug. "You're going to crawl into bed and get a good night's sleep, and then tomorrow, you are going to tell me every single thing that happened to you. And I mean everything!"

"Yes, ma'am," I said.

"It will surely be an interesting story," said Grandpa. "And I would surely like to hear what Reenie has to say, Mitzi. That girl gets around a lot more than we give her credit for."

Mom looked up at Grandpa.

"I guess you're right, Grandpa," she said. "We really were hearing things after all."

Cheng Du, China
by Pat Matthews

Evening weaves a symphony
Mozart couldn't dream.
Notes and tones and counter measures
radio television stereophonic surround sound
that should be cacophonous
but isn't.
Dim damp air resonates
to the sound of busses cars honking horns
flowing in a river of rhythm and rhyme
so glad to be heard
it claps at its own performance.
A song made in America
lifts off the vocal cords of a Sichuan woman
melts runs slips
into traffic and laughter.
A dog yips.
Melodious strains of love and loss
drifting bursts of anger
pass through this night dark space
of teeming music.
One moving composition
the song of life.

Free to Be Me
by Linda Morrow

We're the Hochelaga girls
With the wind in our curls,
And our colors are green and white (green and white!)
We're straight as a young pine
With plenty of sunshine
And our smiles are polished and bright.
We know no weather can faze us,
No feats can amaze us,
We're tops in the sun and the rain (in the rain!)
Because we're stronger and tanner
Than any big towner
'til the mountains fall into Champlain again
'til the mountains fall into Champlain again
'til the mountains fall into Champlain, splash, splash.

July 4, 1957. Warm rays of sunshine caress our shoulders as we march in ragged lines six abreast, wearing forest green shorts and white blouses. We sing in unison and wave at the onlookers lining the main street of South Hero, Vermont, located on Grand Isle, one of several islands in northern Lake Champlain. It's a Camp

Hochelaga tradition to participate in this annual celebration. There is no place I'd rather be.

Like many of my friends, I'd already spent two summers attending a local day camp in our seaside town south of Boston. But during the winter of my seventh-grade school year, I heard girlfriends talking about going to various sleepaway camps. One night at dinner, I brought up the topic.

"Diana is going to go to a camp in Vermont this summer," I said. "I'd like to do that. Do you think I could?" When my parents asked me if I had a specific camp in mind, I shook my head, but I knew right then they would tell me yes!

"When we get the *Boston Globe* this Sunday, why don't we look in the advertising section for some camp listings?" suggested Dad. "Then you can send for their brochures." He paused. "You'll need to find one that's not too expensive. We'll put the day-camp tuition toward the cost, but you'll have to save up money, too."

Of the camps I contacted, Hochelaga, owned and operated by the Vermont Council of the YWCA, was by far the most affordable—$80 per two-week session. I immediately wrote to my grandmothers requesting camp money instead of gifts for Christmas and my birthday. By early spring, I was signed up for two weeks, beginning in late June.

Finally, summer arrived. Sunlight slanted through towering pines, and puffy white clouds hung in an azure sky as Mom, Dad, and I drove past two stone pillars marking the entrance to camp and were directed to a space in a meadow where numerous cars were already parked.

A bit stiff after the seven-hour drive, I climbed out of our Ford station wagon. "Welcome to Hochelaga!" said a young woman dressed all in white. "My name is Janice, but everyone calls me Jan."

I spoke up and gave Jan my name. She ran her eyes down the list on her clipboard. "Ah, you're on the Middler Tent Line. I'm one of the junior counselors assigned to that line, so we'll see each other often. But first, you and your parents need to go to the lodge to sign in." She pointed to a large, two-story, dark-stained wooden building. A series of massive, hinged weather shutters, each held up with a hook, revealed a bank of windows overlooking the sparkling waters of Lake Champlain.

Paperwork and medical review completed, we returned to our car, where Jan stood waiting with a two-wheeled wooden pushcart. "Let's wrestle your trunk on here, and I'll take you and your folks to your tent."

On a path through a pine grove stretched a line of large canvas wall tents, each resting on a pine platform. A horizontal ridge pole held up the roof, secured in place by two upright posts whose iron-spiked tips poked through the peak grommets. Hemp guy lines with wooden tensioners stretched the sides taut. The flaps at the front of each tent were rolled back and tied open.

Jan stopped in front of one platform and lowered the handle of the cart. "Here we are," she said.

I looked inside and saw that three of the four iron cots were already made up.

"I guess you know which bed is yours!" she grinned. "I'll let your parents help you get set up. Then you should all go to the flagpole we passed. Someone will be there to take you on a tour of the camp."

With a wave and a flip of her shoulder-length hair, Jan set off back down the path. I smiled and released a breath I didn't know

I'd been holding. I felt an immediate connection with Jan. She seemed a little older than me and already felt like a friend.

Dad and I slung my trunk onto the platform and shoved it to the foot of the naked cot. I flipped open the latches, and Mom helped me pull my sheets, pillowcase, and two wool blankets from the bottom. Together, we made the bed.

Shortly after completing the tour of the campgrounds it was time for my parents to leave. Dad seemed to wipe something from his eyes, and both enveloped me in a long hug before getting in the station wagon. Brimming with anticipation, I watched the car disappear around a curve, then turned and stepped into the two most amazing weeks of my young life.

I soon realized there wouldn't be enough hours in a day or days in the two weeks to do everything I wanted to try. Camp life centered on the waterfront, which sat below a twenty-foot bluff accessed by a wide stone staircase. Three wooden docks formed an H, and beyond the docks were several floats, including one equipped with low and high diving boards. Aluminum canoes and a small fleet of Sailfish boats were beached to one side of the swimming area along with two wooden rowboats.

We had mandatory swim lessons every morning. A natural athlete, I was pleased when I tested into the advanced swimming group. Land classes included archery, tennis, nature skills, softball, basketball, and a sport I'd never seen before—fencing! A two-story craft house offered painting and drawing, basket weaving, and metal, leather, and gimp work. Vermont clay was used in the lower-level pottery workshop. There, campers could make original creations or paint pre-formed items, such as mugs, and fire them in the camp's kiln. Dance and drama classes in the wigwam rounded out the camp's offerings. The wigwam was a large structure that sat at the top of a hill overlooking the entire camp property with a stunning view of the lake and distant mountains. So many choices! So many new things to try! I signed up for canoeing, archery, tennis, nature club, crafts, and fencing. But camp was so much more than the chance to learn new skills or improve on familiar ones. Camp life provided a simple and predictable rhythm that was very different from my laid-back life at home. From Reveille at 7:15 a.m. to Taps echoing through the camp at 9:30 p.m., my days were full and stimulating. I was never bored. Thanks to the camp's extensive library, located in the lodge, even rest hour became something I relished. Each evening, the entire camp trooped up the hill to the wigwam for our evening program, which was held in the large, open space punctuated by a massive stone fireplace.

Hochelaga gave me the freedom to connect to myself and other girls in ways not always possible in the real world. Here was an opportunity to be anyone I chose to be. As evidenced by the classes I picked, I totally embraced my tomboy, sports-loving self. Ethnic or racial diversity was non-existent and not something I thought about. Most Hochelaga campers came from Vermont. That made me a bit of an outlier, and I came in for some good-natured teasing about my Massachusetts accent. It was fun—I kind of liked the attention I got.

The senior counselors were a more disparate group. These women were from various states, and many attended well-known colleges. They were encouraging, nurturing, and skilled in their specialties.

Jan patiently taught me how to make my bed with neatly tucked-in hospital corners. One of the waterfront staff always stood by the tag board at the top of the steps leading to the lake. "Tags!" she'd remind us. "Don't forget to turn your name tag. White before entering the water. Back to green when you come out." Twice a week at supper, a counselor stood at the entrance to the dining hall in the lodge to collect our "meal ticket"—the required letter home to our parents. When I told the counselor who ran the nature club I'd never built a fire, struck a match, or baked a cake in a reflector oven, she replied, "Don't worry, I'll show you how." The day it was my turn to be part of the flag raising or lowering crew, a counselor stood nearby to ensure we performed the ritual correctly. Every woman was a role model. I wanted to be just like them.

All too soon, my two weeks at 'Laga came to an end. Like many other girls waiting for their parents, I was a puddle of emotions—anxious to see my folks but dreading the moment when I would leave camp and my new friends behind.

"I don't want to go home," I whined as Mom and Dad wrapped their arms around me. "Please, can't I stay longer?" But I knew the futility of my plea.

I'd not had a moment of sadness while away, but once home, I suffered from "camp sickness." My bedroom held no joy for me. I longed for the company of my tent mates. I missed listening to the rhythmic drumming of raindrops on our canvas roof and the haunting trill of loons on the lake. Mom insisted that all my clothes be washed "right away," so I inhaled the lingering smell of woodsmoke from the last campfire before handing over my flannel shirt. The toast I made for breakfast seemed mundane compared to the "doughboys" cooked over open flames during nature class. Even our bathroom smelled "wrong" when contrasted with the musty, wet concrete floor of the washroom. Family meals were far too sedate without the lusty singing that burst from the dining hall each time the counselors and campers gathered to eat. And on Sunday, when I attended church with my family, I pictured Hochelaga's outdoor chapel, where a fieldstone altar stood under the natural arches formed by rows of Tamarack trees. Their fallen needles made a soft ground covering to sit on during the nondenominational services the oldest campers planned and carried out for us.

The next year, by hoarding my babysitting money (I was paid twenty-five cents an hour) and taking any odd job I could, I saved enough to convince my parents to let me attend the entire camp season—eight long, glorious weeks. I spent the next three summers at Hochelaga on the Senior Tent Line, located on the hill between the lodge and the wigwam, guarded by a row of stately poplars whose leaves shimmied in the gentle breeze rising from the lake. A highlight was swimming in the camp's Water Ballet, a Hochelaga tradition, presented at night under lights for parents and townspeople. I learned to scull with my hands underwater to propel my body forward or backward. With the eggbeater kick, we rose out of the water in unison to collarbone level, holding there so that it looked effortless. As with fencing, the tomboy was learning graceful movement.

One summer, along with five other senior campers, I climbed Mount Mansfield, the highest point in Vermont. We stayed overnight in a summit cabin, waking to a sunrise nothing short of spectacular. Another time, I joined a flotilla of canoes on an expedition to the northern end of Lake Champlain. We started with breakfast in Vermont and ate lunch on a beach in New York. When thirsty, we dipped our tin cups in the lake and gulped down the sweet, cool water. By late afternoon, we reached our campsite in Canada. We slept in bedrolls on springy moss-covered ground under shimmering stars, lulled to sleep by the sound of gentle waves breaking on the shale beach. I couldn't believe my good fortune.

In 2019, Hochelaga celebrated its 100th anniversary. Much of the camp property—the lodge, wigwam, and chapel—remains unchanged. The tent lines, however, have been replaced by rustic eight-girl cabins. And while the lodge still resounds with singing during mealtimes, some aspects of camp life look quite different. Kayaks and paddle boards have been added to waterfront activities. Land sports now include disc golf, soccer, and axe throwing. Also new are a camp garden and a wellness program that offers journaling, yoga, and cooking lessons focused on healthy eating. Performing arts activities now include set and costume design.

The greatest transformation, however, is in the demographics of the campers and counselors. The current website describes Hochelaga as a "girls+ space," welcoming girls, transgender, and nonbinary youth. International counselors lead Brazilian dance, Mexican culture and South African beading. "No Bunk Empty" is an initiative to get children in foster care to camp. I am immensely proud of Hochelaga's inclusivity.

Sixty-nine years have passed since I last turned my swim tag or watched sparks dance in the night sky from a campfire at Hochelaga. But the inner strength gained from being part of a community where girls and young women were seen, heard, and valued remains a vital core of who I am. At camp, it didn't matter what your father did for a living or where your mother shopped for clothes. No one cared if I had a boyfriend at home or what grades I got in school. In this intimate environment, I had no fear of being judged. Camp was my safe place. While no two summers were alike, I felt each was a chapter in the same book. Friendships made at camp lasted decades. I followed Jan to college at Syracuse University, and she was a bridesmaid at my wedding.

Now in my twilight years, many of my closest camp friends, including Jan, have passed on. I reside in the Pacific Northwest, thousands of miles from the magical place of my youth. But my camping memories remain undimmed. I still catch myself humming the song we sang in those Fourth of July parades. I'm a Hochelaga girl forever.

Tanka Sequence
by Linda Conroy

two days from town
a time to rest
in comfort of the ocean's ways
its patience
its insouciance

pen and paper in a pocket
ocean splashing at my toes
a memorable escape
lifting daydreams
from the rippling tide

Winter Hummingbird
by Victoria Doerper

February is the longest month. Maybe not in days, but in cold and dark. On the north coast of Washington state where I live in Bellingham, winter lingers like a bad cold. And this winter's darkness infused me with darkness. I'm a walker, through every season and weather. I live near woods, trails, and the Salish Sea, so walking brings me into the community of trees and birds, and this winter, I could see many of them struggling through the dark, wet, and frigid season, too.

On the last day in February, raw and overcast, I ambled along my usual gravel-trailed route down a slope past winter-ragged blackberry thickets, wind-tattered wild rose bushes, scruffy cedars and firs, and leafless alder and maple trees. Birds dashed and dropped through the undergrowth. Juncos. White crowned sparrows. Chickadees. I continued through the dog park, past the deserted heron rookery, past the ill-smelling Post Point wastewater treatment plant. More sparrows and juncos in the rain-trampled verge next to the trail. An occasional great blue heron or red-shafted flicker in the trees. But no hummingbirds. Usually, a handful of hummingbirds inhabits the area, and during the late summer and in autumn, I'd sometimes see a male Anna's hummingbird, his magenta hood sparkling in the sun, perched in a hawthorn tree on the shore of Post Point Lagoon. But through the bleak days of November, December, and January, I'd glimpsed not one whir of tiny green wing. I hadn't seen him at all since the end of autumn.

Anna's hummingbirds here don't necessarily migrate to warm, blue-skied climes to escape the rigors of winter like their rufous hummingbird cousins do. Over the last few decades, the range of Anna's hummingbirds has expanded up the coast as people more reliably supply food through nectar feeders in their yards. I myself was a conscientious nurturer. Nectar tubes always filled. Fresh tubes supplied on subfreezing days when temperatures froze nectar within an hour. A heated feeder on the back deck. Many hummingbirds now remain through the dismal winters of the Pacific Northwest, flashing jewel tones into yards water-colored in rain grey, cloud grey, mist grey, dusky grey. And many continue to live solely in the wild, gathering sustenance from insects, spiders, and winter-blooming flowers.

On summer and fall days, I'd been cheered to glimpse that jaunty male bird out in the wild, so self-contained, poised on his favored tree, often singing. This winter, his absence worried me. I didn't think he'd migrated south. And the winter had been a hard one. Blustery. Wet. At times snowy and subfreezing. For days and days. Weeks and weeks. Months. Even the hummingbirds in my yard seemed to be struggling. But this guy down by the lagoon, how did he manage?

Then again, how do any of us manage in a difficult and stressful time? I wasn't lacking in food or shelter, but my frame of mind was deteriorating with my husband's deteriorating health condition. The stress of caregiving was taking a toll on my health and energy levels. Discouragement swamped my thoughts. Walks in the fresh air, despite cold and wet, brought me the company of creatures who simply went on about their business as best they could despite their difficulties, with no complaining or rumination. And the hummingbirds? There was something special about the hummingbirds—tiny, sparkling, doughty beings who seemed to live on the thin fringe of survival during the winter and still manage to sing.

On that last day of February, I stopped to gaze at the hummingbird's favorite tree, the bare winter-brown hawthorn on the edge of Post Point Lagoon. The afternoon hovered in cloud-cloaked grey light, and my emotions were an exact match. Dark and dank and unrelenting worries bore down. I needed to see the hummingbird in that leafless tree. A spot of uplift. But if he hadn't migrated, he'd probably succumbed to winter's brutal blows and was most likely dead. But maybe not. So, silly as it was, I began a monologue. Out loud. "I'm worried about you. I hope you're okay. Where are you?" As if my human words could be spirited through the air to that tiny being who either was or wasn't still alive. Nothing. And then I wondered if I could call to him in hummingbird. Their vocalizations vary from high-pitched warbling notes to clicks. The closest I could come was to click. So I began clicking. For a minute or more, my tired tongue protesting. *Click click click.* Nothing. *Click click click.* Nothing. *Click click click.* Waiting. Waiting.

And then, under that pewter sky, he swooped in like a bright green comet and landed at the top of the gawky-branched hawthorn in front of me. I drew in my breath. He paused there, facing me, his feathers bringing light on that dull day. Emerald. Ruby. Watermelon tourmaline. I couldn't believe he'd responded to my clicks! Hadn't he? Yes? No? Didn't matter. I was amazed. Shocked. Gobsmacked. I thanked him, shared my relief, wished him health and happiness, shared my hope that when spring came, he'd find a lovely female to make a sweet nest with. And at that moment, he soared high into the air, made a quick U-turn, and returned to his branch. He didn't click but sang in high-pitched warbling. I looked down to check my watch, and when I looked up, he was gone. I'd needed that flash of joy, a spark of exuberant life amidst the drear and drudge. I was grateful. But I didn't expect it to happen again.

The next day, I walked to the tree, paused, and clicked. And, unbelievably, he flew in again. I had no nectar to tempt him, nothing at all to entice him. And, clearly, I was not a female hummingbird offering up her charms. But still, he appeared with my greeting, perched on a slender branch, and sang. I stood silent at the lagoon's steel blue waters and thanked him from my quieted heart.

Day after day, in clear, cold weather, on overcast days, in wind, in rain, in warming sun, he swept in when I clicked a greeting. Around day ten, I began to depend on his cheerful presence as a joyful moment in my day. I wasn't sure why he came when I clicked. I didn't always wear the same jacket, nor did I visit his tree at the same time of day. I offered nothing but gratitude and some measure of interspecies friendship, but what could that mean to a hummingbird?

As the days warmed into March and spring began, with its tender unfurling of buds and call to new life, he still appeared when I clicked, but his visits became shorter. On a few days, he treated me to the dramatic Anna's courtship display, flying so high into the air that he became a speck and almost disappeared, then rocketing back toward earth, feathers whistling in his descent, before looping up abruptly and landing again on his perch. Some days, he'd whir quickly away in the company of a female hummingbird. He dazzled and gladdened me.

And then, on April 3, after thirty-three consecutive days, he disappeared. On that day, I thought he might be somewhere off with his mate. Maybe on the nest. Feeding young. Did the males feed young? I hoped he'd be back soon. But, day after day, I called to him and he did not appear. I walked on, feeling bereft. I continued my usual daily walking route, clicking beseechingly, careful as I'd always been not to display my odd behavior as other walkers passed by. Two weeks after the hummingbird's disappearance, as I stood in front of his tree, a friend I hadn't seen for a long while walked by. We chatted, and she asked if I was bird watching. A little sheepish, I told her about my experience with the hummingbird, speculating that those days of magic may have simply been coincidence. She told me she didn't believe in coincidence, gave me a hug, and walked on.

The following day, I paused once again at the tree and clicked, expecting nothing as I stared into the vacant air. And then he astonished me by swooping in and perching on a budding branch. Long enough for me to gaze for a moment, thank him, and say goodbye.

In the months and months since then, I've stopped by his tree and called to him, but I never saw him again. But he'd made it through that winter, and so had I. And though I still miss seeing him on my walks, I hold him in my mind's eye like a flickering candle flame cupped against the wind, a cheering light I keep for other dark times that will surely come my way again.

A Triplicity of Interior Alaskan Moments
by Susan Chase-Foster

A mischief of half a dozen
boisterous black-billed magpies
sweeps through peeling paper birch
and naked aspen.
Swashes of pitch-dark caps,
snow-white chests,
teal-blue wing tips,
fickles of flakes
on long wedged tails
whose shadows momentarily
mottle snowdrifts,
then dash on as if chased
by sundogs.

Iksgiza Lake,
one of three million mirrors
in this place of sky, clouds,
ice fog and rainbows,
of black spruce,
listing log cabins,

and tundra swans circling,
as we are in a bush plane
when the pilot grunts
"Not good!
Which is the sky?
Which is the reflection?
Should we ask a swan?"

At Circle Hot Springs
we shape our wet hair
into frozen Statue of Liberty
spikes, and trot toward the cabin
wrapped in wool blankets
in lieu of fur. Above us,
Lady Aurora sky-dances
in her shimmering chartreuse,
violet and carmine gown,
while we twirl, spin, swirl,
moose-moan and wolf-howl
like those we hear around us
from our holy, euphoric tribe.

Tennessee Farm Roots
by Cynthia Mitchell

Granddaddy was born Lonnie Tyler Mitchell in Hancock County, Tennessee, in March 1909, with no birth certificate or record of an exact date. Grandma Hazel Belle Miller was born in Kyles Ford, Tennessee, in July 1908. So far east and north that Kentucky and the Virginias are an easy reach. Fully grown, Granddaddy stood five feet six inches and weighed in at around one hundred and twenty pounds. With Grandma—all five feet eleven inches and about two hundred and fifty pounds of her— the two of them made an amusing Jack Spratt couple. Grandma told me she'd been afraid to marry someone large, lest they have giant children.

Tennessee sure suited me, planting the seeds of faith and intuition that guided and grounded me throughout my life. Most summers, our family—Mom, Dad, older sister, and younger brother—would drive from Texas to Tennessee for a week's visit. My earliest memory of Granddaddy and Grandma's farm, a hundred acres from the top of the ridge to the middle of the creek, is walking beside Granddaddy down to the barn at milkin' time, with the peace fingers of my left hand hooked in the pant leg loop of his overalls, the one carpenters use for hanging a hammer. With

Granddaddy somewhat small in stature, I must have been not more than a toddler to reach up like that. Me and Granddaddy. I followed along anywhere and everywhere he'd let me.

Grandma Hazel had two large gardens—both were the "you name it, it's growing" kind. Summer vegetables outside the back kitchen door, clothesline bordering one end with berry brambles up the T-post. Root and vine fall vegetables across the road, above the ice-water house that held one or two milk cans for pickup by the local milk distributor, in front of the tobacco-drying barn. Squashes and pumpkins, white and sweet potatoes.

Grandma could hoe a row like nobody's business. Hands the size of dinner plates, gray hair in a bun, sweat-stained bodice, splatters and grime on a threadbare cotton print dress with a cotton slip beneath, deep-pocket apron around her large girth. Always a wicker basket alongside with a small paring knife to snip okra, no bigger than your little finger. She had a keen eye for the yellow-striped, green tomato worms that could strip a large plant in no time. Pluck from deep inside a jungle of vines and fruit, toss to the ground, hoe in half.

My grandparents visited the closest town, Surgoinsville, infrequently. Grandma canned and froze produce straight from the garden and orchard, had chickens that provided eggs and an occasional Sunday roasting hen, kept about a half dozen cows for milk and butter, and let roam their small herd of beef cattle in the hills.

They were more vegetarian than not, the midday dinner table laden with palm-sized, thick-sliced heirloom tomatoes of variegated colors, yellow, red, pink, and brown. Green beans round and slender, flat yellow butter beans, shelled lima beans, peas. Okra, sliced in thin, half-inch rounds, cornmeal-coated, fried and fried and fried some more in the cast-iron skillet on the left back burner next to Granddaddy's white-enamel red-trim coffee pot.

More okra boiled up whole. Spicy-bitter collards and mustard greens. Corn—creamed, cut, on the cob. Sliced cucumbers and butter pickles. Gritty cornbread and flaky buttermilk baking-powder biscuits, fresh warm or day-old cold. Cream gravy made by stirring a large spoonful of flour into the hot skillet of bacon drippings till brown, then adding two cups of milk, bringing to a simmer, and stirring till creamy tan. Bacon grease in everything.

From the fridge, Grandma's churned round of butter, covered in perspiration as it warmed to the room. Cow milk, warm and fresh, or cold. Buttermilk to finish off a meal, a large glass with crumbled cornbread: spoon it.

And always a berry cobbler made in a nine-inch square Pyrex, Grandma's special recipe. Melt a quarter cup of butter in the baking dish, stir in a mix of flour-sugar-baking powder, layer on warmed berries coated in sugar. Bake until the buttery flour mix bubbles to the top in mounds of golden-brown crust around pools of thick berry juice.

I loved going down the steps to the musty, dank, sour-smelling unfinished basement, framed at the far end by a large garage door left open during the long, hot, and humid summer days. Keep my eyes on the steep wooden stairs, the creaks familiar with each step down, left hand trailing the wall. There are beds in opposite corners of the basement. My grandparents preferred to sleep here rather than in the three bedrooms upstairs. Country folk keep those rooms nice! Clothes cleaned in the large, white enamel-tub wringer washing machine. Flattened clothes drape high to dry over wires strung wall-to-wall. Newspapers on the floor against one wall strewn with large, bulbous white and yellow onions, their long green stalks turning brown.

There was a large chest freezer packed full of fruits and vegetables and ancient packages of meat, often spoiled with freezer burn. Cobwebs and interesting spiders lived here, and shelves of ancient blue Ball jars with the old-style metal rings and glass lids, the dust layered thick, the contents a decaying brown. It was a mystery how old they were, why they'd never been touched, what was in them. During my summer visits in my teen years, I emptied the contents a few at a time into the compost pile out back. I took the jars home with me, wrapped thick in Granddaddy's old overalls—fashion-fodder for my denim hippie wardrobe.

Grandma was a root doctor. Many folks sought her out for advice on lingering illnesses. Although she was never called to set bones, she knew what to do for the accompanying swelling and how to hasten the healing. She was just as good with animals. On seeing a milk cow in the pasture all bloated after eating too many apples from an overhanging branch, she grabbed the kitchen broom and announced, "I'll just go stick this handle down her throat." The cow was fixed.

Early morning and late afternoon was milkin' time. Granddaddy would push the wood-frame wheelbarrow cradling the empty ten-gallon milk can *bang clang* down the rough, rutted path to the ancient barn held up by hay bales. In the cool barn, light filtered through cracks and gaps in wall planks, the air thick with the dust of hay and dung. It always took a few moments for my eyes to adjust. Grandma would come down from the house or out of the garden, and together they milked. Each had a three-legged stool and a cow-kicked stainless-steel milk bucket held firmly between splayed knees. The top of each of their heads pressed into a cow's right flank, a left leg and upper arm bracing the hind leg of the cow to keep her still. Right-hand fist punches up in the ballooned udder. Pull down on the right outside teat, and encircle at top with thumb and index finger, high up. Then, one at a time, the other fingers close, squeeze, pull down for the steady milk stream, *phish, phish.* Repeat, again and again, all four teats till the udder hangs loose and low, deflated.

Fields on either side of the cow barn were a luscious mix of pasture topped with cow-graze manure. Green as a smell, not a color. Fresh, celery crisp, photosynthesis and chlorophyll, minty, astringent, acrid. Large, layered cow patties dry, decompose, flake open to reveal a host of worms, maggots, fly larvae. A resinous decomposition. The smell of grass and manure intertwine and weave together, heaven and earth.

Late in the day, far north of the kitchen garden, a cold, wet wind surges with the advance of black, blue, grey clouds barreling down the small, sheltered valley—known in Tennessee as a "holler." I have one hand on the clothesline as cotton print dresses and denim overalls flap and twist; my hair is blown straight back off my face. My eyes pinch, my heart sings. "It's coming, it's coming, rain is coming!"

While I was in college, my grandparents died and the family farm was sold. I married in my late twenties, and with our own home, my husband and I took up backyard gardening for the fun of it, to see what could grow, to have something to do outside. Fifteen years later, in a bigger home with two young boys and a bigger yard, I turned to the garden for emotional support and comfort. The garden as a mother who always loves us. I walk back and forth. Back and forth. Right foot, left foot, barely lift, small forward step. Head down.

The husbandry and thrift of the farm had spoken to me. To use and reuse—not just once or twice, but again and again and again—like a clod of soil in Granddaddy's hand; open palm, squeeze fist, crumble, and sift through fingers. Dirt falls on thigh, toe of boot, open furrow. Matter returns to the source. My approach was to ground down. Be connected. I needed to harvest edibles from the earth. I needed to stoop-bend-kneel and pinch-pull-pluck. Green aliveness, divine photosynthesis, sun to sustenance, straight to my mouth, dirt and all. Green of fertile energy, sustainability, and peace. Green as yellow trial of faith mixed with the blue healing power of God. Green as the color of relentless desire. I needed to go beyond nutrition to refection— to the restoration of mind, body, soul. My summer vegetable garden was not enough. I wanted a year-round garden even in my town's cold and snowy winter. I needed what only this precious earth could give: to persevere and endure, to revive and renew.

I was in a workhorse marriage, raising my darling sons, prone to carrying the world on my shoulders. I was the household manager, gardener, financial planner, bill payer. I was bringin' home the bacon with a high-powered career, trying to change the utility industry from consumption to sustainability. More cases, more hearings, more airplanes.

My husband and sons converted a little-used, south-facing grassy area outside our walkout daylight basement. They constructed three twenty-foot-long, four-foot-wide, one-foot-high raised beds, bordered on each end by concrete retaining walls. With full sun exposure in the winter, the retaining walls provided radiant heat and protection from cold winds. We rigged up a simple greenhouse from hoops of curved, half-inch PVC pipes planted every six feet and covered in greenhouse-grade plastic held in place with large plastic clips.

I grew greens like nobody's business—arugula, dandelion, bok choy, chard, kale, red-striped and speckled lettuce. I tended to soil health and was rewarded with earthworms and bugs. A salad-plate-sized toad took up residence in the bed against the house. I named him Mr. Toad and crowned him the garden caretaker. Spring through fall, Mr. Toad covered his body with a thin layer of soil, keeping his head partially exposed. Come winter, Mr. Toad burrowed deep down to hibernate. Come spring again, greeting Mr. Toad, I felt transported into Kenneth Grahame's *Wind in the Willows*.

I fell in love with the sharp, complex, bitter, and very earthy kale—queen of the cruciferous vegetables, a family of superfoods packed with nutritional and health benefits. Kale was heartier and more resilient than other vegetables in that family—cabbage, bok choy, broccoli, brussels sprouts, and chard. Kale held its ground against often crippling infestations of aphids, white flies, and pill bugs, growing (more slowly) during the winter and producing a decent second-season crop. So many varieties to choose from! Curly Green, Lacinato (or Dinosaur), Kamome (or Ornamental), Redbor, Red Russian—I grew them all. Year-round greens, combined with summer-season tomatoes, peppers, beans, squashes, and a stand of fruit trees, reined in trips to the grocery store. I avoided the endless aisles bursting with plastic-suffocated fake foods and largely foreswore beef. I picked up Michael Pollan's palm-size book *Food Rules* and decided to put it into practice, starting with Rule Thirty: "Eat well-grown food from healthy soil."

By now, I could trace twenty-five years of utility advocacy, starting as a high school graduate sitting in regulatory proceedings over skyrocketing utility bills after the 1973–74 OPEC oil embargo. Increasingly, my work of truth and right against the utility companies' lies and wrongs felt like two steps forward and one—or more—steps back. I was bolstered by the garden.

Early on as a child and teen, it was a curiosity and fascination with the foods my grandparents grew and put up; skills passed down, practiced, and refined season after season. Later, as a young woman, then wife and mother, growing and preserving food was my foundation of home. My grandparents' Tennessee farm also gave conviction to my lifelong career spent trying to change the utility industry's business-as-usual approach that didn't seem to care about the fossil fuels they burned or how much they contributed to global warming. As an energy economist, I testified in state electric utility proceedings around the country, shredding some of the biggest utility bullies in the industry, being cross-examined by some of the tightest sphincters on the planet. I cultivated a family garden as an antidote to the exhaustion of my David and Goliath work. *Garden* as a verb; active and never finished.

Many years earlier, my toddler son, in his cousin's hand-me-down lacy pink sleeper jammies, chinned up on the second story windowsill of his bedroom, little fingers pressed into the ledge, and gazed far afield through valley dusk. He said, "Momma, most people don't take care of the land." Stretching further up on tippy toes to look directly down into our vegetable beds, he continued, "But you do, Momma, you take care of the land."

I recalled my grandparents and whispered, "I am trying, child, desperately trying."

My Sacred Temple
by Susan Griesen

My Sacred Temple is crumbling
Forty-five years of yoga have forsaken me
I can no longer do the full bridge pose
Even though I did it once correctly

My wrists don't flex
My back won't bend
My neck is tight
My groins don't extend

Has my yoga ship sailed?
Is it perfection I seek?
Yoga was once my salvation
But now my muscles are weak

Hip and wrist arthritis
found a new home in my joints
Once soothing yoga poses
have become sore sticking points

Child's pose now hurts
Downward dog requires props
I can't hold most poses for long
Let me finish and lie like a corpse

Secretly I admit the sole reason I go
To seek my luxurious retreat
The sauna melts my aches and pains
They love the nurturing heat

My yoga instructors gently
Guide me through the routine
I listen to their messages
Some that are not always obvious or seen

I was surprised one day by the question
"What do you want to keep?"
"Compassion and love" are what I found
When I looked deep

Gradually I awakened and discovered
My yoga buddies I didn't always see
I rarely noticed their impact
Their collective positive energy

Some with healing fractures, chronic arthritis,
Joint replacement, or cancer mayhem.
Their diagnoses make me seem young
Yet they never let it bother them

During our yoga practice
We are not to look and compare
So, what am I moaning about
Thinking life is unfair

Many in my classes are older than me
Some a decade or more
We have known each other for several years
Next to them, I lay my mat on the floor

Steph and Karen in their upper seventies
Pat and Jim in their eighties, and Jane is eighty-nine
I covertly look for them during my practice
Whenever I want to moan or whine

Dementia has a grip on Sonia at eighty-two
A caregiver guides her poses
Once a European child of war
Her smile is like a bouquet of roses

Robert, eighty-four, limps in with chronic pain
Carolyn battles her third cancer at eighty-two
They are my chair yoga buddies
My self-gratitude is way overdue

I modified some of my poses
To not cause so much pain
This change to my practice
Is for those who are more sane

Maybe I'll complain and feel sorry for myself
But only for a moment
Because I will look for my yoga buddies
And banish my sorrow and judgment

My yoga family inspires me
They have shown me this is just another stage
Because of them and their guidance
My Sacred Temple is full of yoga that doesn't have an age

Baghdad Diplomatic Guard Rules of the Road
by Kenneth Meyer

That Sunday in late August 2003, Security Officer and Diplomatic Guard Lewis Cager exited the interior of Saddam's Republican palace in Baghdad, now the Central Command of Coalition Operations. The structure lay east of the 14 July Traffic Circle, on the west bank of the Tigris. He stood in the enclosed, marble-surfaced, air-conditioned foyer and greeted Corporal Ramsey, the marine standing in the plexiglass, bullet-proof cage. Ramsey controlled the electronic locks to the doors entering the palace.

"Beautiful day in the Bagh, Rams."

"Yes, sir, it is."

"Another run to the airport," advised Cager. Ramsey probably already knew that, but you made small talk.

"Safe journey, sir."

"Thanks." Near Cager's right wrist was a ceramic urn that at one point may have contained a plant. Whatever was in there had been uprooted, perhaps thrown into the river—uproot the government, tear out the plants too! Now, embassy wits placed their umbrellas in the urn, because occasionally there was rain. Cager went his colleagues one better and placed the vinyl sleeve containing his M4 rifle with scope in the receptacle. While he waited, he pulled a dog-eared, coffee-spattered paperback out of his suit jacket pocket, the memoirs of the scholar and one-time ambassador to India, John Kenneth Galbraith.

Cager read: "It's problematic to argue for extensive help to, or military backing for, a state where the central government doesn't even control the route to the main airport."

Goddamn right, thought Cager.

He was halfway through Galbraith's autobiography. Cager wasn't a political analyst or an area specialist—those were the prestige jobs at embassies and missions around the world—but he was capable of learning. In his opinion, everyone better be. You lived longer that way.

He remembered there had been a portrait of Saddam in the main foyer. In that oil painting, the leader was in a green field marshal's jacket, glaring at the viewer—perhaps about to ask, "Did you interrupt me?" An affirmative answer usually resulted in the death of the respondent. That painting was torn from its frame and lying on the marble floor by the time Cager arrived in May. He remembered the curious fact that in all the ripped-down portraits and posters of Saddam he had seen around the city, there wasn't ever one of the leader reading a book or writing anything. There was orating Saddam, Saddam with a rifle, Saddam riding a horse like a medieval Arab warrior, Saddam in a suit, Saddam wearing the traditional Arab headscarf, a *keffiyeh*, Saddam raising a fist, Saddam lifting a sword, Saddam with his arm around a little girl—but no Saddam with a book or writing. Cager believed it was telling.

Williams, Cager's partner for the day, entered the foyer, also in a suit. He carried his long gun in an identical vinyl sleeve and chewed an aromatic piece of bubble gum. In most locales, diplomatic guards like Williams and Cager carried sidearms only, but this was Baghdad.

Each diplomatic mission abroad housed an assortment of personnel from different agencies and departments. In the case of U.S. embassies, the personnel included men and women from the intelligence elements, Defense Attaches, Legal Attaches (usually FBI), officers from USAID, the U.S. Information Service, and so on. Since the components of the mission included personnel from different agencies and departments, the diplomatic escorts and guards were also from different elements. Cager was former U.S. Army but now associated with the CIA. Williams was regular State Department, a former police officer. Just as each mission was under a State Department Ambassador, the guards and escorts followed the direction of a Regional Security Officer, always a State Department career officer. All of these people of different backgrounds and talents were expected to function together as one big family, and for the most part, they managed to do so. "We're on the same team," some fool always said at meetings.

"Williams, ready? Two vehicles and four escorts will do the necessary today." Cager replaced the battered paperback in his left suit jacket pocket.

"Ready, Team Lead."

These were formulaic phrases. On each sortie of the guards and their charges, there was always a Team Lead, who would take operational command in an emergency. Today, that was Cager. The two men escorted visitors and mission personnel around Baghdad outside the Green Zone. Hearing that there was a Green Zone, or "safe" zone, was comforting until you found out ninety-nine percent of the country was the Red Zone, where anything could happen. The Green Zone was about the size of four baseball diamonds. That was why visitors and mission personnel needed armed guards. The more, the better.

At this stage of the allies' involvement in Iraq, the mission wasn't going "full battle gear," and Cager was wearing an unremarkable gray suit with body armor underneath. The outfit was bulky and constricting, but Regional Security Officer Lane said the customers would be less spooked that way. Cager believed the people he escorted were already scared enough, especially after the August 19 assassination of the U.N. representative in Iraq, Sergio Viera di Mello. At this point, Cager, age thirty-five, had been deployed in Kinshasa, Algiers, Freetown. "All the joy spots," he would say.

"She's right behind me," advised Williams.

Cager replaced the paperback in his jacket pocket and picked up the sleeve containing his long gun. "We'll wait here for her." Because it was 119 degrees Fahrenheit outside, stepping out there was like jumping into a heated pool.

A woman in a white raincoat clutching an attaché case entered the foyer. This was Jennifer Hawks, an economic officer returning to Washington. Cager couldn't help thinking, *Ma'am, it's sunny and 119 degrees out. Next time, lose the raincoat.* Hawks was either very pale or scared to death. So much for Lane's breezy remark on keeping the customers relaxed.

"Good morning, ma'am. We're your escorts for today." The three exited the foyer into the bright sunshine and found two Chevrolet Blazers retrofitted with armor idling before them in the midday heat. In the first vehicle, "Cheetah One," sat one passenger, a State political analyst named Green, Security Officers Murray and Cesar, and the driver, Sami, a local employee of the mission.

Why two vehicles for only two passengers? Experience had shown that despite all precautions, one vehicle could break down, be disabled, hit an improvised explosive device, and so on. So at least two vehicles went on every sortie.

"Let me get the door for you, ma'am."

The three people climbed into Cheetah Two. Cager went around and sat on Hawks' left on the rear bench, behind Hassan, the driver. Williams sat on the front bench, on Hassan's right.

Cager explained to Hawks: "This will be the same as last time. I'm Officer Cager, in case you forgot." And of course she would have. "Sitting up front is Officer Williams. If there's trouble, follow my direction. Otherwise, you won't hear from me."

"Got it," said Hawks.

The two vehicles rolled down the drive and carefully navigated the six concrete barriers. The metal quarter-cylinder lowerable car barrier slid down, and the front gates of the palace swung slowly open. Cheetah One eased out the gate.

"Cheetah Two, we're on our way," reported Sami from Cheetah One over the speaker on the dashboard.

"Copy that," said driver Hassan in Cheetah Two.

"ETA in twenty minutes," said Sami.

Cheetah Two followed through. The airport was sixteen kilometers west of Baghdad.

There was little traffic, and the scenery along the four-lane highway to the airport was monotonous. Sandy neutral ground flanked the four lanes, and three hundred yards away, on either side of the road, rose six- and eight-foot-high walls of residential compounds, some painted white but most an unadorned gray. No pedestrians walked alongside the highway, and there were no sidewalks, either. Cager kept an eye on the walls of the compounds on both sides of the road. No one would be reading paperbacks for the next twenty minutes.

They had just passed the eight-kilometer marker when Sami in Cheetah One reported over the intercom: "Taking fire."

"Active shooters on the right," added Cesar in Cheetah One. "Two o'clock." It meant there was some kind of firestep behind one house's wall, and the hostiles leaned their rifles over the wall, shot, and ducked down again.

Cager looked to the left. There would logically be shooters there, too: no action. He extended his hand over the seat, and Hassan passed him the mike. "Sami, punch it and let's get out of here."

"Vehicle is hit," reported Sami.

"Keep going!"

But the lead Blazer slowed, shuddered, and came to a full stop.

"Obstacle in road. I don't know what. Vehicle immobilized," reported Sami.

Fuck. Hassan stopped Cheetah Two behind and to the left of Cheetah One. The first vehicle was now between Cheetah Two and the unknown attackers.

The first rule that informs incident response, which any idiot can grasp, is that attackers will hit you at their prepared spot, called X. Your imperative is to get off X. If your tires are shot, run on flats. As long as the engine is running, get off X. If you have to, get out of the vehicle and run for cover, away from X.

Cager looked left. Still nothing. Into the mike: "Sami, call it back. Request helo support."

"Yes, sir."

Cager to Williams: "You ready, buddy? Keep down, ma'am."

"Ready."

No further communication came from the occupants of Cheetah One.

Trained attackers would fire from two separate locations, but that wasn't happening. Of course, two or three men firing from one location was bad enough. A helo gunship would be on the way, maybe arriving in twenty minutes.

Cager again took the mike from the driver. "Cheetah One, everyone prepare to exit on your left side and come to our vehicle. Move when I rap on your window, and bring your gear." Meaning, leave no weapons behind. "Acknowledge."

"Roger that," said Cesar in Cheetah One.

Rule two of incident response: You don't exit your vehicle and start blasting back at attackers. That only happens in movies. But in this case, Cheetah One was immobilized. *We have to get out of here*, thought Cager. *We'll take a risk.*

Rule three of incident response: Armored vehicles are only designed to take the first two or three rounds from long guns, and you don't even want to think about rocket-propelled grenades, or RPGs. If you're under attack, don't sit in the armored vehicle sticking your tongue out at the bad guys. Bullets will eventually come through. Which takes you back to rule one: Get off X.

Cager asked again: "Active shooters?"

"I count two. Still at two o'clock," reported Cesar over the intercom.

Another indication that this was amateur hour: after the initial attack, they should change position.

Cager instructed Williams: "We'll take cover behind Cheetah One and lay down fire. We get our people over here and leave Cheetah One behind." To Hawks: "Ma'am, we'll be right back. Stay down. Williams, on my mark." In unison, Cager and Williams slid their M4s out of their sleeves. "One, two, go!"

Cager exited the left side of the Blazer and sprinted to Cheetah One near the driver's window. The heat was draining. A brief glimpse of Sami's face, and Cager motioned for him to get down. Three feet to Cager's right, Williams fired at the compound.

Cager heard the attackers' bullets *zing* by an instant before the report of the rifles. He saw two heads and rifles bob up behind a wall on the right, three hundred yards away. The hostiles fired, then the heads dropped down again. To Williams: "I see them. Take the one on the right. When I say 'now,' we'll pull out Green and the others."

"Affirmative."

Cager fired twice at the left hostile, but no go. *Loving my scope,* thought Cager. He took another shot. *Did the distant figure twist away clockwise? Did I hit him?*

"Now." He rapped on the window of Cheetah One, and the doors opened. Cager had his left hand on the neck of passenger Green, bending him over as they ran. Williams fired three more rounds.

Doors opened at Cheetah Two, and bodies piled in. Williams, Cager, and Green were on the front bench of Cheetah Two with the driver. Sami, Murray, and Cesar squeezed onto the rear bench with Hawks.

"Hassan, go!" The Blazer leaped forward. "Anyone hit?" Negatives all around. In forty seconds, Cager's suit had become soaked with perspiration.

"Hassan, faster." To the passengers: "It's over. Eight minutes to the terminal. We're all okay. Sorry about the cramped ride."

No bullets hit the vehicle as it sped away from the Kilometer Eight marker. The rebels had had enough for today, and Cheetah Two was quickly out of range.

Cager turned the car mobile set to channel eighteen and took the microphone. "Checkpoint Six, this is Cheetah Two. We're coming in with all passengers accounted for. We had hostile contact."

"Copy that."

Checkpoint Six was the entry point for Baghdad International, at the end of the sixteen-kilometer highway. It consisted of a cinderblock tower and concrete barriers a vehicle had to slow down to navigate. Next to another lowerable car barrier stood Corporal Fuchs, USMC, whom Cager also knew. Overlooking this array of barriers, stood six serene palm trees, three on each side of the road. They had somehow survived the last four months of war.

When the Blazer pulled up to the lowerable barrier, Fuchs— eyes invisible behind his dark glasses—motioned for Hassan to open the driver's side door a crack (otherwise you couldn't hear anything). Cager leaned across Hassan.

"Sir, where's Cheetah One?"

"We had to leave it behind. But we have all personnel accounted for."

Another marine ran the mirror under the vehicle.

Fuchs: "Do you require medical attention?"

"Negative."

"You're clear. I'll tell you when to proceed."

The barrier lowered.

Cheetah Two proceeded to the Departures drop-off. "Cesar, Williams, take our M4s and wait for us at Arrivals. Murray, you and I will accompany to the departure gate."

The interior of the Baghdad airport never failed to impress. The ceiling was an assembly of illuminated domes, reminiscent of an Abbasid dynasty mosque or palace. Saddam had not stinted on its construction and design. It was undamaged. And it was even better now that it had Starbucks and Pizza Hut.

At Departure Gate A-18, Green said nothing, but Hawks, her complexion now a normal hue, handed him something. "This fell out of your pocket."

It was page 143 of Galbraith's memoirs, with a clear heelprint on one side. "Thank you, ma'am."

Hawks nodded slowly, but whether it was in approval of his reading matter or his thanks was indeterminate. "Get back safely," she said.

"We will, ma'am."

Then the two travelers were gone.

Cager exhaled, carefully wiped the page on his jacket sleeve, put it back in its correct place in the paperback, and replaced the book in his damp suit pocket.

John Kenneth Galbraith. That guy knew stuff.

Seaside Snapshot
by Linda Conroy

We build castles,
trusting in this stretch of sand and time,
these waves, tiny, in a wrinkled sea.
Gulls peck and squeal, swoop,
our distant sentries on an empty plain.

My back is to you as I shape a trench.
I don't remember this event
or you so young, so cute, hands turned out
pausing, posing
as if to say "who, me?"
A bandage on one knee,
wind in your face,
eyes scrunched to peeping slits
as your mouth grins.

I don't remember when you looked
as if at any moment you might dash
and giggle, splash into a rush of fun.
Was happiness a distant holiday
or was the twist of wind
a lavish choice, a bridge across a moat?

Young as we were,
fresh, in this sublime scene,
I didn't think time would run out.

The Mountain
by Judith Shantz

I never would have believed it then, if someone had told me that going up would be the easy part.

I had donned cheap Army-Navy Surplus boots and an even cheaper backpack and set out to haul forty-five pounds up the side of a mountain. After half a mile, I was certain that I couldn't do it. However, with my more adventurous companion's verbal prod, "Of course you can," I slogged on for another grueling five hours, too embarrassed to admit defeat. My backpack dug hot pink ridges into my shoulders and hips, and my toes slammed into the ends of my ill-fitting boots. With my eyes fixed tightly on the path immediately before me, I almost missed the little sign with a tent symbol and an arrow carved into the wood. To my right was a pretty lake with several tents pitched along the edge. The trees had thinned perceptibly, revealing the towering mass of the Olympic Mountains. I was exhausted! I was exhilarated! I had made it four miles up that mountain.

I had been hauling a different kind of baggage when I first arrived on the West Coast. I was a child of the fifties, raised in a very conservative and reserved society; a girl who always did her homework on time and taught Bible stories to little children at church on Sunday mornings. When I traveled, I wore a skirt and jacket, and sometimes even a hat. I had never owned a pair of jeans.

As I lurched into the sixties and young adulthood, I found myself in an exciting world exploding all around me, opening to infinite possibilities. The wounds of the previous war were scarring over. Our generation could go anywhere, do anything. I was quite sure that I could braid the values and beliefs of my childhood into a new, progressive cloth—the best of both. I had met and married a good man who shared many of my aspirations, so I tossed out the hat and bought flip-flops and blue jeans. I door-belled for politicians, I recycled newspapers, I hugged trees. Until, of course, it all started to fall apart. Until our young men were sent to Southeast Asia to die. Until our folk songs became anti-war anthems. Until our heroes were assassinated. Until that good man turned out to be the wrong man.

I, too, was wrong. I had not been successful at interweaving my strengths and beliefs into the new fabric of late twentieth century life. Instead, I had been peeling them off like pieces of sunburned skin. And with them went some of my sense of what constituted family, loyalty, and religious belief. I had whittled Christianity down to stewardship and community. I left the physical church behind. But in all of that, I also lost my youthful self-confidence and sense of purpose. I felt lost, lonely. What had once defined me seemed to be crumbling away.

I wanted to believe that two roads had diverged and that I had made conscious and informed choices about which to follow. One road would lead to renewed determination, to gather the pieces, to make it work. The other would lead to something new. I had gone back to school and made new friends and suddenly realized that I had made my decision long ago. As I watched a midlife birthday approaching from over the horizon, I knew I needed to create my own future. I knew which path I had already chosen.

This was neither a beginning nor an ending. It was more of a middle, a pivot point. I was encouraged by family and friends, adventurous ones who were also looking for new ways of living in the world—active and invigorating ways.

I started by becoming a runner. Not quite abruptly, because I was very sure that no ordinary mortal could really run more than half a mile at a time. But one winter day, when no one was around to watch me, I put on my old pair of Sears Jeepers and managed to jog three-quarters of a mile through a light snowfall. That was the beginning. Then, day after day, year after year, I ran through failure, heartache, fear, and success. I fled panic attacks on foot, running the high school track and the nearby trails. I pounded pavement before the sun came up. I built muscles and lung power and confidence. A perfect fit. The only prerequisite was a decent pair of shoes. I could run with friends or alone. I could run at any time and on any route. My only coach and taskmaster was me. By the time I first climbed those mountain trails, I was unencumbered by most of my old, preconceived notions and creeds.

I was, however, covered with blisters. Fortunately I had brought extra socks, and those were stuffed under the offending straps of my pack and into my sloppy boots. I went on. Over the years, the equipment improved, and I got stronger. My backpacking companions changed as children grew up, I remarried, and some of my friends grew older and frail. We planned more ambitious trips: longer, weightier. They never got any easier and not long ago, they began to get much harder.

Toward the end of one hike, as I was starting to retrace my steps, I stopped to look down the sweep of mountain below me. I felt a catch in my throat, as I always did, and a sting behind my eyes. How could such immeasurable beauty exist? How could I be someone so blessed by its embrace? I heard the crunch of boots on the path behind me, and I stepped aside to let a younger, stronger hiker pass me by. But he didn't. He stood aside for a moment, a young man, short and muscular with a shock of straight, black hair standing up in the wind. He spoke one word very softly, as though I wasn't there: *"Milagro."* Then, for my benefit, "It's like a miracle." I agreed, a miracle.

Long after he disappeared down the trail ahead of me, I began, slowly and hesitantly, to sing "Father, We Thank Thee," a simple hymn that I had taught to very young children at my church when I was not much more than a child myself. After all the years of inquiry and questioning, I returned to this simple hymn. Gratitude for letting me live so long in paradise. Gratitude is my religion now.

My father revered the poem of a fellow RCAF pilot, John Gillespie Magee, who had died young, and who had written, "I've. . . put out my hand, and touched the face of God" after he had soared thousands of feet above the earth. I may not have soared, but I have climbed. There is neither creed nor dogma that could replace this green distillation of creation, this deep bowl of an inverse heaven, sweeping out on either side and a thousand feet below. The sweet grey-green lake tucked halfway down on a ledge, reflecting the lowering sun, and the occasional black bear loping across the meadow below me, are all the paradise I need and all I can put my faith in.

Now, in the night, I often awake in panic and it takes some minutes to settle my mind on my distress. The great sorrow of one's own demise? Well, of course, that is part of it. The pile-up of myriad regrets? Yes, that too. But perhaps it is also the fading away, the diminishment of my senses and abilities.

And, largely, it is the loss, the never-again-ness of it! Would I ever again be able to stand in the cool afternoon air rising from the valley, shaking out my little yellow tent, that gossamer piece of net and nylon, and watch the breeze and the sun catch it before I pinned it to the earth? Would I never again lie in the grass to see at eye-level the dozens—no hundreds—of avalanche lilies caught waving in the morning breeze or hear the bugling of the bull elk as they bring their harems up past our camp on the way to the ridge above us?

I have hiked and climbed in several mountain ranges, but there is one place to which I return over and over. There's a shrub, or a clump of heather, high on the facing wall of scree. Year after year, its shape has remained the same, that of a bear cub clinging to its mother. It must be very large as it is easily recognizable from across the quarter-mile expanse of the cirque. Will that be the last memory I will have—clinging? So reluctant to let go?

I know now how I wish to be. Accepting. Grateful. Will I be able to push my longing through the slough of my despair, to the other side, to the place where memory is etched on the backsides of my eyes, never to fade? The one where ache becomes a blessing? Where I can embrace my waning years as a chance to express gratitude to whomever or whatever God may be?

Forest Music
by Taya Sanderson Kesslau

In the sun-drenched forest
when the air is dripping with stillness
the robins circulate their juicy songs
echoing here and there high above
in audible lines of community.

On rays of sunlight like waves
over an ocean of evergreen
glad music drifts
down through the canopy.

Droplets of symphonic light
feed every nook of life
all the way down to the earthen floor.

Alaskan Encounters
by Sheila Dearden

Over a hundred years ago, European settlers in the Pacific Northwest told of salmon runs so thick it was possible to walk across rivers and creeks on the backs of fish. Today, those runs have declined precipitously, impacted by what fish biologists call the 4Hs: habitat loss, hatcheries, harvesting, and hydroelectric dams. Every year, as I watched the remnant populations of spawning salmon on the local creek close to my house in Washington state, I tried and failed to imagine a stream flowing with more salmon than water.

I would only understand the abundance that had existed for thousands of years and register the extent of its loss when I travelled to Alaska for the first time with my husband and our two young children. We stayed in Wrangell, a small town in the Southeast Alaskan archipelago. Eager to see salmon and bears, the information center informed us that Anan Creek Bear Observatory, located thirty miles south of town and only accessible by boat, is one of the best places to visit. Two days later, we were seated in a small, flat-bottomed boat as our guide steered a course across a shallow bay to the rocky shoreline fringed with forest, nudging the bow against seaweed slick rocks long enough for us to scramble out. We waited in the shade while he secured the boat, returning minutes later, a rifle slung over his shoulder. At our look of alarm, he reassured us with a smile, "We're required to carry a rifle as a precautionary measure against potentially aggressive bear encounters. I promise you, I have worked here for many years and have never needed to use it."

Gathered in the cool green shadows of the immense trees, he explained that the Tongas National Forest, at 26,100 square miles, is the largest intact temperate rainforest in the world.

"The boardwalk we're following has been built to protect the banks of the creek from erosion. Rainfall is measured in feet, not inches, around these parts." He laughed. "Roughly four feet annually, so the ground can get pretty churned up. The overlook at the falls where we're heading is about a mile upstream."

He turned, and we followed slowly, only to halt after a few minutes as a black bear with a salmon clenched between jaws crossed the boardwalk some distance ahead and disappeared into the dense vegetation. We watched wide-eyed, children and adults alike, as our guide whispered, "We'll just stay quiet and wait here for a few more minutes and give the bears plenty of space."

I pressed a hand to the dry, scaly bark of a Sitka spruce and peered up the length of its trunk to where the crown was lost in a snarl of branches and needles mining meager sunlight. Lichens of all shapes and sizes draped over trunks and branches. Velvety mosses claimed what space was left. Fungi pushed up from the earth, spilled along nurse logs, or sprouted step-like up the sides of snags. These giant trees would be the envy of any engineer tasked with the design of a structure that could withstand the extremes of battering storms, heavy rain, moisture-laden snow, and the desiccating heat of summer months. These trees had been nurturing life long before the European settlers arrived. Sentinels to the ebb and flow of water in this tidal estuary, proffering shade to spawning salmon for thousands of years.

A beetle stirred the moss in the crevices of bark beside my outstretched palm. Spider silk stitched a silvery sheen over the scaly roughness. From the branches overhead, I could hear the gossiping chirps of a flock of kinglets as they gleaned insects hidden within chinks of bark, moss mats and needles. A solitary tree creeper was on the same quest, tiny feet scratching a purchase on the scaly bark as she pecked a path up the trunk. She paused, cocked her head. In stillness, her brown-gray mottled feathers became bark. Old needles, moss fuzz, and specks of lichen dislodged by the birds drifted to the forest floor, adding to the layer of detritus, destined to be spun into compost gold by a factory of decomposers.

"Scoop a handful of topsoil," our guide explained, "and in the palm of our hand we will hold life: arthropods, some smaller than the period at the end of a sentence, together with the tissue of plants, mosses, fungi, bark munched by the jaws and guts of millions of bugs to release stored nutrients back into the system."

We started walking again, only to stop a few minutes later as another black bear climbed across the boardwalk ahead of us and made his way down to the creek. The ranger pointed to an alder tree below. Dirt had been scraped away from its base, the culprit revealed in the bear-sized teeth and claw scrape marks on the exposed roots. White filaments like cotton threads were stitched throughout the exposed soil. He explained that the soil contained fungi whose slender hyphal threads intertwined with the roots of trees to create a complex, interdependent, mutually beneficial network connecting life to life. A forest ecosystem that functioned as a single vast living organism.

The sound of splashing drew our attention to an opportunistic seal chasing salmon on the incoming tide beginning to flood the braided creek. Brackish water lapped at the forested shoreline, the musk of tree resin and damp earth blending with the briny scent. A bald eagle flew low over the water, tracing its course upstream. We continued along the trail to the viewing platform adjacent to where the creek narrowed and tumbled over boulders, creating a series of waterfalls over which the salmon had to leap. It was an ideal fishing spot for black and brown bears. All around us were well-travelled bear trails through the dense vegetation, littered with the chewed remains of salmon carcasses they had dragged from the creek, the air ripe with the pungency of decomposing fish.

Walking at the back of the group, I lingered over the remains of a salmon on the boardwalk, its brains and roe removed with surgical precision. Impulsively, I slid the tip of a finger into one of the large punctures left by the clamp of a brown bear's canine, imagining hot bear breath and jaws containing teeth larger than the diameter of my index finger. My ten-year-old daughter turned at that moment.

"Mom! What are you doing?" She hissed. "Now you're going to stink of dead fish, and there are bears everywhere!"

I stood, a naughty child caught in the act, mumbling apologetically, "I wasn't thinking, but I'm sure it'll be okay."

"That's what you always say!" Eye-rolling as she stomped away, leaving me to wipe my fingers furtively on a fern frond.

A photo blind had been built at stream level, and our family tiptoed down the wooden steps to the lower platform. Within moments, a large brown bear ambled from the trees on the opposite bank and waded into the living river of salmon no more than eight feet from where we sat breathless with excitement, peering through openings in the wooden screen. Hardly able to register our good fortune, we watched as he hooked salmon from the water with a paw larger than a dinner plate, tipped with curved claws, each one the width of a man's finger and easily the length of a hand. Feasting on the brains and roe of the salmon, he discarded the remains for the eagles and ravens perched in the surrounding trees. Finally, satiated on salmon, he lumbered back into the trees. Within minutes, two black bears emerged from the shadows, a mother and her yearling cub, judging from his size. Effortlessly snagging a fish, the mother bear carried it up the bank, leaving her cub hunkered in the creek and staring at the salmon through the curtain of foam. We couldn't help but laugh at his futile attempts to bat the water, hoping to snag a fish with his paw. After several minutes of exertion, he clambered up the bank to follow his mother into the forest.

Further upstream, the creek widened into shallow riffles, forcing salmon to shimmy over a gravel bar. Two juvenile bald eagles, feathers mottled with the grays and browns of spruce bark and water-washed rocks, were perched on a low snag to watch as a third young eagle danced clumsily in the shallows, stirring the water with a taloned foot in a vain attempt to pluck a fish. Once again, we couldn't help but chuckle. With such an abundance of fish, this was the perfect foraging place for young, inexperienced hunters to hone their fishing skills.

We stayed at the creek watching and marveling until dense clouds squeezed out the late afternoon sun, shutting in shadows among the trees. The tide was beginning to turn, and with it the eagles and bears, out to the estuary where salmon were forced into narrow ribbons of creek drained by the outgoing tide. We followed slowly in the gathering gloom, pausing several times to give space and time to black bears crossing the trail ahead of us.

A few days later, we left Wrangell and traveled north by ferry to the small town of Petersburg. Waking early on our first morning, we headed to the harbor to meet up with the captain of a small fishing boat repurposed for whale watching.

"We're heading to Frederick Sound," the captain yelled over the rush of air as the boat skimmed over the milky flat expanse of sea and the glint of a pearl sun. "It's an important feeding ground for the humpback whales that spend the summer here."

We could only nod in acknowledgement, mesmerized by the scenery sliding past us. A glacier-sculpted landscape painted every shade of gray and green by ice-born fjords and forests; rounded tops of rocky outcrops, more like giant turtles than islands, dotting the coastline.

A movement on the nearby shore caught our eyes, and the captain idled the boat so we could see a shadow emerge from the trees and flesh into a black bear who ambled to the water's edge, nosing for crabs among the rocks. And then, with the distraction of children at an amusement park, our heads turned to the sound of whales. Whale breath mingled with misty tree breath over the silvered sea as we held *our* breath to watch three humpback whales, curved backs, notched dorsal fins, and tails in the shape of hearts pulled wide, slide into a deep dive.

The boat captain lowered a hydrophone overboard, and for ten minutes, we listened to nothing but the lapping of water and the occasional shriek of a gull. Abruptly, the stillness was interrupted by a one-note whale call followed by a second single note rising in intensity. A flock of gulls took off from the water and spiraled overhead.

"Watch the water for a ring of bubbles where the birds are circling," the captain urged. No sooner had he spoken than the surface roiled and belched out whales with cavernous jaws wide, throat pleats distended, and water foaming from their mouths, squeezing excess saltwater through their baleen plates as they gulped mouthfuls of churning herring. Gulls swooped and snatched at stray fish amid the feeding frenzy. Sixteen whales, with the combined tonnage of a modest-sized cruise ship, wallowed on the surface, rumbling calls of satisfaction like the bellowing of elephants before sinking beneath the water on a last inhalation of breath. Gulls bobbed on the eddying footprint left in their wake. Stillness was restored. Pearl-blue water and forest green came back into focus. The four of us on the boat looked at one another, let out a collective breath of amazement, and burst out laughing. Did we just see that?

"What they're doing is bubble-netting," the captain explained. "It's a cooperative hunting strategy unique to humpback whales. The group dives deep below a school of fish, herring in this case, encircling them and swimming upward in a spiral while blowing bubbles from their blowholes to coral the herring within a net of bubbles. That single-note call we heard was from the leader signaling to the group it was time to force the fish to the surface. They might resurface again soon."

Minutes later, the hydrophone whistled into life with a humpback whale's haunting, single-note song. Loud enough, the sound became distorted, and the hydrophone cut out. The whales were so close we could hear their call resonating through the aluminum hull. We scanned the water, hoping not to find ourselves surrounded by a ring of bubbles. Our boat was little more than driftwood to a large group of humpbacks preoccupied with bubble-netting herring. Despite the urgency of the call singing through the hull, there was nothing to see. I envisioned the scene unfolding below us as we listened to melodic instructions from one individual in the group, choreographing this dance of whales and herring. Five hundred and thirty tons of muscle, blubber, sinew, and bone, circling, blowing a net of bubbles to corral herring into a tight ball, forcing them to the surface.

Suddenly, there was a flapping of gulls, and my husband yelled, "The front of the boat!" as the humpbacks burst to the surface in a rush of water and sound, just fifty feet off the bow. They were close enough for us to see the fringed baleen plates lining the roof of their mouths, the smell on their breath a stench like that of fish long past its sell-by date. A group of Steller sea lions lunged on the edge of the feeding frenzy to snatch at escaping fish.

We spent the afternoon in the company of humpbacks until, replete with herring, the whales dispersed—our cue to head back to town. Within minutes of starting the engine, black fins sliced through the water toward us. We leaned over the edge as far as we dared to watch a pod of Pacific white-sided dolphins surf in the boat's bow wave. Their slick, streamlined bodies slipped through the water, twisting on their sides to glance up at us, seemingly as fascinated by us as we were captivated by them. Eventually, they too disappeared one by one into the gray-green depths of Frederick Sound. Our family leaned into one another on the boat as it sped back to land, our words and thoughts blown away on the wind as we held tight to wonder and astonishment of this beautiful world.

Near Whatcom Falls
by Shoshana D. Kerewsky

A Muscovy duck,
beak skyward, guzzles rain, fills
up, stoneware pitcher.

Crocosmia bright
to my right. I write. Wasps bomb
from their paper nest.

I like this walk, but
I long for conversation,
Not this long silence.

Thirteen Ways of Looking at a Place Called Mexico
by Jes Hart Stone

I am falling in love. Bewitched by brown-skinned boys racing scooters, smitten with girls decked in flowing skirts and embroidered blouses, charmed by elderly men singing love songs as they sweep dusty streets. Wooed by the fragrance of roasting chickens and fried tortillas.

I travel by boat, plane, and automobile to coastal villages and towns high in the Sierra Madres. I stay in pueblos with names I can't pronounce and in cities featured in classic films. I drag my little dog along, and sometimes, when I'm lucky, my buddies Pam and Melanie join me.

Pam and Melanie are smart and gutsy—great traveling companions. And, because they are vacationing and I am relocating, they give me their luggage allowances. The dog and I are moving to Mexico, two suitcases at a time.

1. The Kindness of Strangers

My bilingual driver, Sergio, waited for me outside the Tequila Bar at Puerta Vallarta's International Airport. We'd never met, but I recognized him from his Facebook photo—his smile wide and bright. Eyes shining, he wove through a crowd of tourists, and though we were only internet friends, he gave me a warm embrace.

"Bienvenida, amiga!" He scooped the dog from the crate and snuggled with my travel-weary pup. He carried my luggage up a demanding staircase and across a footbridge to his air-conditioned car. On the drive to the Airbnb, we laughed and shared life stories.

The Airbnb was locked. Sergio banged on the gate, pounded on doors, and rattled questions to neighbors in Spanish. The landlord was absent. The afternoon turned to twilight, and twilight grew dark.

"Sergio, I feel guilty. I only paid you to drive me here, and this is taking so much of your time."

He gazed down the shadowed street, up the crumbling buildings, into the night sky. Then he looked at me and said, "Amiga, I will never leave you in danger."

Three years have passed, and he still picks me up at the airport, drives hours to rescue me when my rental car gives out, waits all day while I deal with bureaucratic business, and finds pet sitters when I need to travel sans furball. He drives me to Costco, teaches me to swear in Spanish, and tells me which cities are safe and which to avoid. Sergio will never leave me in danger.

2. The Mysteries of Mexican Food

Some travelers use their phones to translate menus into English. I want to learn Spanish, so I risk ordering with the point of a finger. One day, I coaxed Melanie to be brave and pushed her to take a chance. So, like me, she pointed to a random item on the menu and hoped for the best.

My meal arrived—a creamy rice dish with six large shrimp, roasted mushrooms, fresh veggies, and a side of fruit. But Melanie's dinner was a charred fish hull, its dead eyes staring in disbelief.

Another time, Pam and I found a thatched-roofed palapa overlooking a crowded beach. We ordered burgers and beer. Our sandwiches included beef, bacon, sliced ham, and salty fries that sent us into a flavor swoon. Later, I ordered a salad—it came garnished with glazed, deep-fried insects. In Mexico, you just never know.

3. Lost and Found in Translation

Pam could order beer, find bathrooms, and navigate GPS directions in Spanish. But Melanie and I were not as savvy, so we downloaded language apps—Duolingo and Babble. As we learned, we traded phrases.

"I can buy a red dress in Spanish," Melanie said.

"Well, I can buy shoes in Spanish," I told her. Two lessons later, we planned a shopping trip.

Before leaving, I tried a new greeting for the Mexican man who mowed my lawn. He was patient and forgiving as he explained that I'd just said, "Good morning, Mr. Goat Head."

I now know how to say, "Please forgive me. I'm learning Spanish." This pleases everyone, from taxi drivers to bank tellers to cleaning ladies. They attempt to teach me new phrases or words. And they laugh with me when I mangle their language. They know I'm trying.

4. Rough Roads and Wonky Wi-Fi

In the villages and pueblos of Mexico, many sidewalks are broken, pitted, sloped, or missing. Cobblestone streets are rutted and muddy. Some roads are wide enough for a Volkswagen bug, while others are four-lane superhighways. Cars can disappear into potholes along the free roads. The toll roads are safe and well-maintained, but don't drive on them at night. It's not about bandidos. It's about wandering cows, deer, jaguars, and snakes—huge, highway-crossing snakes.

In my small village, the internet works most of the time. Except when it rains. It rains for two hours every evening. Read a book.

5. Living a Full Life with an Empty Wallet

Canadian and American dollars are worth more than Mexican pesos—even when the exchange rate changes. And the exchange rate changes every quarter hour (or so it seems). My friend Bob watches it with the intensity of a day trader. The dollar is up—the peso is down. Or the other way around. The Mexicans don't seem to care. Neither do I.

I know how to ask what something costs, and in fact, my accent is almost flawless for that question. Sadly, I don't understand the answer—ever. I'm terrible with numbers. I give shopkeepers a paper bill and hope it will cover my purchase. They smile and give back change. I know it's correct.

The expats whine about prices going up. They lament the good old days. But a hearty dinner here is the price of a latte in Seattle. Manicures are eleven dollars, pedicures fifteen.

6. The Hardest Working People on the Planet

The lady who cleans our four-story townhouse charges the equivalent of thirty dollars per day—she cleans for five hours with no breaks. The house sparkles when she's done, and then she goes on to clean another gringo's house before heading home to cook for her family.

It's too hot for me to go to the beach. Too hot for my little dog to walk—even under the shade of the palms lining our street. On the way to my air-conditioned home, I pass a group of men constructing a cement building. They mix the cement by hand in a sloppy pile on the ground. They shovel the heavy mixture onto concrete blocks and smooth the gloopy mess with trowels. Everything is done by hand—in the sun. The men sport ratty straw hats and tie cotton bandanas around their necks. They wear jeans and work boots.

A child lugs a plastic pail of water from man to man. Each worker pauses, dips a communal cup into the water, drinks, and then pours a few drops on his bandana or under his hat. He returns the cup and goes back to work. The child struggles with his load as he goes to the next man. These men and this child will be here until two, pause until four, and then work until sundown. They started pre-dawn.

7. Mexican Time

Time is fluid in Mexico—the hour of an appointment is more a generality than a commitment. Public events do not start at the times stated on posters or websites. Stores do not always keep regular hours or even open on regularly posted days. This can confuse tourists and newly minted expats, especially when making appointments or hiring workers.

To most gringos, the term *mañana* means "tomorrow morning." As in, "I'd like you to do the job mañana—tomorrow morning."

But for Mexicans, *mañana* means "not right now."

"Yes, I'll do the job for you. Sometime. Not right now."

8. Above Everything, Love of Family

On Sunday mornings, large families—twelve or twenty people—rent tables in front of restaurants on the beach. They spend the entire day at their table, eating, drinking, and laughing. Too bad if a group of random tourists wants to stop for a bite or cool drink. They won't find seating. Sundays are family days.

One Sunday, Pam and I lucked out and managed to squeeze into two seats at the end of a family's table. We ordered margaritas and listened as the adults joked and chattered. We watched teenagers flirt and children chase gulls along the shore. One diapered toddler wandered away from the group and stumbled toward the water. Pam and I jolted—alert. Baby in danger. The other adults didn't seem to notice. The toddler wobbled across the hot sand and almost reached the shoreline when a teenage boy leaped from his seat and sprinted down the beach. Scooping the child up, he lifted the laughing babe high in the air. Cuddling and cooing to the child, the teenager rejoined the others. No stress. No trauma. Family.

9. Of Saints and Fiestas

Hugo is my Spanish teacher. He charges two hundred pesos an hour (about ten dollars) to teach gringos Spanish and Mexicans English. I'd probably be fluent by now if we'd stuck with the language lessons, but Hugo is keen to introduce me to his culture.

He tells me tales of ancient tribes and how the Mexicans conquered them. He tells me stories about the Spanish and how they conquered the Mexicans. And he describes how the Catholic Church conquered everyone.

When the Spanish and Christians arrived in Mexico, they stole land and temples from the indigenous people. Hugo wants me to see one of these ancient temples, so we drive my Jeep into the hills. At a crumbling stone structure no bigger than a one-car garage, we meet the present-day guardian of the temple, an elderly Catholic priest.

The small, dark building houses a collection of statues—virgins, saints, a couple of Christs. After describing each sculpture, with Hugo translating, the priest blesses me . . . twice. Hugo is sure the priest will be sainted someday, and he says I am lucky to be blessed by a future saint. Maybe the priest guesses about my college days and figures I need a little extra help.

We discuss festivals—not just the big ones like Easter and the Day of the Dead, but the hundreds of little ones celebrated by each village and pueblo. People are proud of their heritage, and weeks before a festival, entire villages flutter with enough crepe paper to decorate a Macy's Thanksgiving Day parade.

10. Rules of the Road?

I know there are rules of the road here, but I don't know what they are, and, to be perfectly honest, I don't think Mexicans know them either.

Pam is a bona fide badass driver. She roars along winding jungle trails, bombs up mountains, and speeds down the highways of Mexico. She weaves around gaping holes, edges past herds of meandering cattle, and passes sixteen-wheelers on two-lane dirt roads. And, like so many native Mexicans, she drives while eating spicy Dorito chips and drinking cold beer.

11. Angels of Mercy

I'm clumsy and uncoordinated, and one day, I tripped, fell, and twisted an ankle. The medical clinic, only a short hobble from the house, was once a cantina—its interior, cool and dark. The one-time bandstand was made of smooth concrete and lined with plastic chairs. I took a seat and waited my turn.

A young man stopped at my chair and grinned. He wrote my temperature and blood pressure on a notepad, handed it to me, and gestured for me to print my name. No English in the clinic that day.

My wait was less than ten minutes. The doc was a willowy woman with shiny black hair and a broad smile. She didn't understand my broken Spanish, but she understood broken bones. She cradled my swollen ankle in her hands.

She handed me a slip of paper, and using charades, she instructed me to take a taxi to the next town for X-rays and to return to her.

The cab driver glanced at the paper, nodded, and drove me to a treatment center, where I paid in advance, in cash, for three X-rays. Five minutes later, limping, I followed a technician down a hall. I left the center clutching a folder of developed film.

Back at the local clinic, I plopped down and waited. Soon, the doctor appeared, grabbed the folder, and disappeared into her exam room. When she returned, she gave me a big hug. Again, with charades and the help of Google Translate, I learned I'd only suffered a severe sprain, not a break. The doctor gave me pain pills and another hug. The entire process took four hours.

Soon after, I sat at a beachfront restaurant with a cold beer. The total cost for the doctor, cab rides, X-rays, and meds was fifty-two US dollars. The beer was a buck twenty-five.

12. The Music of Mexico

Mexico is a noisy country. Roosters, dogs, firecrackers, and church bells herald the dawn. Babies wail, neighbors call to each other, police whistles scream. Speakers mounted on trucks blast messages—*gas for sale, water for sale, ice cream, pastries, vote for me!* Bands of musicians roam the beaches, serenade city parks, and practice their tunes on buses.

Near farmlands, you hear goats, cows, and coyotes. Next to the jungle, it's monkeys, parrots, and trillions of insects. The sounds of Mexico are a symphony of life.

13. Enchanting Confusion

I don't know if it's because I don't have enough Spanish yet or if it's just Mexico, but even simple tasks seem cloaked in chaos. While there are scads of rules and regulations, there are workarounds for everything. And nothing makes sense—or at least not much.

For example, if a store clerk doesn't have the correct change, you might get pesos and a handful of Chicklets. Pills prescribed by your doctor are poured from a large bottle into an envelope. A nurse or high school kid will print your name on the envelope, or they might just tape it closed and hand it to you.

You can receive major medical attention in an afternoon, but getting a driver's license can take three months. National Guard troops look fierce as they ride in their big trucks, dressed in camo and holding automatic weapons. But they grin and wave and call silly greetings to my little dog.

Like a child, I am constantly filled with bewilderment and awe. At some point, every day, I wonder what in the world is going on. I ask my Spanish teacher about all of this. Hugo simply smiles, shrugs his shoulders, and says, "It's Mexico."

When I Die
by Beverly Ott

Lay my perfectly spent
profoundly loved and wrinkled
life-worn body that created wonders
back down where I started

Lay me in a peaceful dell
with my face to the sun and stars
and cover me in a cotton cloth
that I may not disturb passersby

Let birds use my wild snowy curls
to soften their beds
and let ants wander across
my gentle peaks and valleys
to find tidbits for their young
and let wild beasts
find sustenance in my flesh
as mushrooms and all that is verdant
thrive on the wetness escaping me

And when my flesh is gone
let porcupines gnaw

my beautiful old bones
let creepy crawly things find shade
beneath them and build their homes
in the nooks and crannies

Lay me down with my mother
from whom I came
who nurtured me
who gave my soul peace
who shared with me marvels of
true beauty

Lay me down with my mother
so I may return life to her
and we can be one
again

Leaving
by Holly Witte

They left the vineyard on a July day with the sun warming the grapes they no longer owned. They had sold or given away all their horses, making sure each one was in a good home and keeping together those that they could. They turned left onto the road taking them away from Oregon's Willamette Valley and never looked back, although she knew they would never lose the picture of it in their minds, that lovely place they had lived in together since their 2006 wedding.

Charlotte, who was driving, kept her eyes on the road, but she was really seeing the pictures in her mind. She thought about the seventeen weekends she had driven there from her Seattle home as the budding relationship with Jim was forming. She thought about how it seemed as if it rained every one of those weekends and that, for the first month, she had to call Jim for directions as she got closer because it wasn't straightforward once she left the freeway.

As she had grown less nervous about getting lost on those drives, Charlotte started looking forward to the way the landscape gave way from the commerce of towns to the open fields of farmland and, finally, to the road leading to Jim's vineyard. As she passed the field on the right where strawberries grew in summer, she saw Jim taking her to pick them there on an early date, and how she had worn city slacks that showed dirt stains on the knees from kneeling to pluck those ripe red hearts hanging from their curling stems. She remembered how luscious they tasted as she ate at least as many as she dropped into a basket, helping her forget the ruined slacks.

As the homes and fields of their neighbors receded in her rearview mirror, Charlotte was overcome with how complete she had felt in that place, in their beautiful house built in a semicircle so every window held a majestic view. She had loved that their bedroom overlooked the lower vineyard, whose seasons she knew so well, from neatly pruned rows lush with green leaves on woody stems emerging from gnarled sculptures of trunks, to a golden fall canopy after harvest, to wavering skeleton limbs of winter. She loved how the morning mist fell over the vineyard like the incandescent brightness of a fairy blanket. She loved how, in the spring, they could see the entire sweep of the nearly five hundred rhododendrons producing blooms as big as their heads that grew up the driveway and around the house.

The leave-taking made her aware of how she had thrown herself into becoming a winemaker's wife, learning the lifecycle of the vineyard as fast as she could, helping to develop the destiny of the vineyard. Jim had planted the vines beginning in 2000 and was living his dream of letting the land do what it was meant to do. Consumed with growing, he hadn't begun to figure out what would happen to all the wine once he made it, giving Charlotte real purpose. It was as if they had come together with each bringing something that would fit into the world of the other. Jim brought the love of the land and how to tend it; Charlotte's skill was bringing people together. He made the wine; she figured out how to let people know the wine was there. Over the years, their tasting room became exactly what she had hoped—a lively gathering place. Guests crowded the bar to sample wines and chat, relaxed on the patio, or sat in the teahouse Jim had built for their wedding, gazing out at the vineyard. The landscape was framed by towering fir trees on one side and blooming cherry trees on the other.

Jim and Charlotte never forgot how lucky they were to have found each other, as loving partners, late in life. It was true they had never lost track of each other, but that was because their group of friends, people who had met decades earlier at the videotape production company Jim was building, stayed in touch no matter how far apart they were. That these two—Charlotte had been Jim's secretary—got together and married was remarkable, exciting, legendary in the company. She had been married to someone else in the company, a man everybody had loved, who had died in 1980. Jim's late wife had been the company office manager. They were entwined. They had history, trust, shared experiences, wonder, and reverence for their love.

It had been a jam-packed thirteen years already. She wished she had been there when Jim planted the first of the vines. At least she had been around for the planting of the youngest vineyard, giving them two blocks of Pinot Noir they named after their dogs, Gemini and Trouble, whose photos appear on the labels to tell the wines apart. They cultivated the grapevines together, with Charlotte lending a hand to prune or pull weeds when the work was too much for Jim and their one full and one half-time employees.

After practicing how to make wine with grapes from the first few years, grapes that are discarded because they haven't begun to achieve character, they found it thrilling to taste the fantastic

2008 vintage and decide it would be their first commercial release. That vintage was extraordinary, rated the best in decades in the Willamette Valley. They were proud that they had recognized it. That wine won awards right out of the gate, the first of their many award-winning wines. They opened their tasting room in 2009, in the daylight basement of their home. Charlotte, who had grown up in an apartment in New York, had never heard the words *daylight basement*, hardly the right term for the lovely lower level of the house that opened directly onto the patio and the vista of the vineyard. They loved every inch of that house, and their many guests loved it. It became a destination.

Along with the achievements and accomplishments, there had been a few catastrophes: Jim, who was accident-prone, had broken several bones over the years, and Charlotte had a health issue surface in 2009. There were two fires—the second destroying their barn and winery. And, now, Jim had been diagnosed with mesothelioma as well as a faulty heart valve. Somehow, though, they took each in stride as the next thing to deal with, making it part of their lives together. This began to mean a diminishing life. Jim couldn't manage the vineyard any longer, and as much as Charlotte was involved, she not only didn't know enough to manage the vineyard but now her full-time job was Jim. It was time to go.

Jim was tentative about leaving, although he loved the house they had bought up at the top of America in Washington near the Canadian border. He hesitated because the heart-valve team based in Oregon, the women and men who had wrapped their arms around this man, had been working for over a year not only to find a solution for his poorly functioning tricuspid valve but also to replace the device they had inserted, which had failed but stayed attached, flying around near his heart. Now they had that solution. Jim and Charlotte were hopeful because why would the team go to these lengths if the mesothelioma was really an imminent threat? Jim and Charlotte believed they had years yet together and that this surgery would give them those years wrapped up in a graceful state of relative health. Still, Jim wondered if they should move three hundred miles away before the surgery.

The timing meant that they would spend that first weekend in their new house and then drive back down to Portland, where Jim would have surgery. Charlotte would go home while he spent ten days in the hospital undergoing post-surgery testing done not only by the medical team but also by the entire pharmaceutical company team, which would be flying in from all around the world to meet Charlotte and Jim and be present for this groundbreaking procedure.

And that is exactly what happened. They spent three days in the hospital room together, with Charlotte sleeping on the window seat bench the night before the surgery and the next two nights. At dinner on the first night, the dietitian who brought their meals asked them if it was a party room. They were nervous but hopeful and excited, allowing themselves to talk about how they would live on the ninth hole of a golf course, looking out at two ponds and, as Jim put it, also at eighty acres he didn't have to care for.

The surgery went amazingly well, with the old device captured successfully and encased as planned and the new device firmly attached to the tricuspid valve. His heart function improved noticeably at the very moment of attachment.

When Jim began to wake up, she was allowed to see him. To her surprise, he had been fitted with an oxygen mask. The two surgeons walked in, and they, too, were surprised. The attending

ICU doctor told them Jim was struggling to breathe and his throat was swollen.

That was wrong on so many levels.

The doctors determined that his throat had been irritated by the camera inserted to enter the chest cavity. They were sure it would resolve.

The next day, he was awake and able to swallow liquids but with difficulty, as if he had the worst sore throat of his life. Still, the valve worked perfectly, and everyone was sure the throat swelling would subside. Charlotte went home, as planned, to unpack.

It was a feverish nine days, but she did it, grateful for activity to keep the worry at bay as the issue with Jim's throat wasn't resolving. He was, however, cleared to go home with a plan for outpatient therapy to treat the swelling and swallowing and to identify the few things he could eat.

They didn't know quite yet that they had been tossed a slow curve ball, one they would not be able to catch. Charlotte was surprised at just how exhausted and discouraged Jim was at the end of that first day at home. And the next day.

The third night, he had a little more trouble breathing, and the nagging pain in his back, the one that had been there for two years and was caused by the mesothelioma, kept him from finding a comfortable position. He had gotten used to the absence of pain after an early course of radiation, so this was an unwanted surprise. He was irritated and frustrated, and by morning, she knew they were in trouble. He was having trouble breathing and beginning to panic, air hungry.

Jim had pneumonia—the first of four bouts. Because of his inability to swallow, even the soup or yogurt that had been cleared for him to eat could sneak down the wrong pipe and lodge in his lungs to fester. Four hospitalizations over the next several months. At least, they could go to the hospital fifteen minutes away instead of having to drive back and forth to Oregon. After the first bout, he was discharged with home health services set up and a nurse who would visit several times a week. Antibiotics were added to the other meds he was taking, which all had to be ground up and mixed with the yogurt.

This was their new life. It was clear that his body was weakening, and his resolve was, too.

Charlotte stops here, at least, for a while. Or maybe she just needs to approach this next part slowly, stealthily, sneaking up on her own feelings. She has already understood about herself that writing her stories is keeping her here. Or, rather, *there*. She has already spent years playing with time, experiencing all time at the same time, watching time being speedy just as her son had once said and she had repeated back to him at his wedding, adding a line J. D. Salinger gave to Seymour at the end of *Raise High the Roof Beam, Carpenters,* that time moves "Quickly, quickly. Slowly." An exquisite line that sums up for Charlotte how much she has done, how fast it has all passed.

How can we possibly measure time passing, anyway? Because it is only the moment we are in that is real, measurable, felt. She can sift through all her important moments and be enveloped by the feeling of being in them when she puts them on paper, or even just thinks about them, tangled in the bedsheets where it is just Charlotte and sometimes a wisp of something she thinks she sees from the corner of her eye. But she isn't really in the moment she is conjuring or that has been assembled for her from the millions of synapses in her brain. She cannot have any of those moments again; none of us can.

So what is time? What is anything? If she stops writing right now, Jim, in an alternate universe, doesn't get the terrible diagnosis, doesn't endure any of the months of his dying, stays alive.

Can she control time? How much of a cloak of comfort can her imaginings produce? She pictures them walking to the rocky beach near their home, sitting together on the peeling bench, watching sea birds, occasional sea lions, little pecking birds among the rocks. Then they go to lunch somewhere interesting, or maybe just to the unpretentious café at the golf course where they live. Maybe they wander home, maybe they garden in the spring, maybe Jim plants a grapevine or two, just because. Maybe Charlotte tends the peonies, the bush she brought from their Oregon home, the same one from which she had plucked the flowers for her wedding bouquet. They would cook together in the open kitchen, having a glass of wine as they fussed, finally sitting down at their pretty table in front of the windows overlooking the pond, on the dance floor, as they laughingly would say, recalling another time, another place.

She knows how it will end and that she is left with nothing if she doesn't commit to, at least, converting the fleeting pulses into something on paper. She has already welcomed into her present so many of the bone moments of her past, letting them sway as if on a cutout paperchain, letting them have residency in her soul, so she knows she will take this last part through to its wrenching conclusion, and maybe then, when there is nothing else lurking or waiting to be revealed, she will find rest.

Down There
by C. J. Prince

the descent into the ragged
    edges of memory
        avoids Dante's door

bare feet and sand
    unseen green glass
        blood on sandcastles

hidden under the pier,
    the kiss, the rape
        fear a trap door to suicide

tear-rivered cheeks
    telling the doctor
        asking, begging, stoic

an abortion, her mouth
    a smoky grate, holding back
        clenching the request

the doctor reversing destiny,
    this woman of hollow cheek
        red-rimmed eyes

she says, looking at him,
    quietly, I won't have this child
        he nods, quick action required

The Breaking and Rebuilding: Reflections on the Jersey Shore
by Michelle DiSarno

A place can be imprinted in your memory even before cognition. It can get absorbed into the marrow of your bones. The memory belongs to my parents first: pushing one-year-old me on the stroller and taking me to ride the carousel on the boardwalk that overlooked the Atlantic Ocean. I don't *remember* this, of course, not really. But the *experience* of it must have seeped in and stored itself in my body. The rhythmic bump of the boards beneath the stroller's wheels, the thrilled screams of amusement seekers, the percolating lights of arcade games, and the scent of fried dough and cotton candy and ocean salt that meandered around in the breeze—how else can I explain why these impressions still produce an aching, ecstatic nostalgia?

More than that, the Jersey Shore was the arena for my childhood, at least for the season that matters most to a child: summer. The calendar was always spinning toward it, sometimes agonizingly slow, as we walked to school with heavy books and heavy looks, slumped in our chairs while waiting out the bland, light-deficient winter. Each Labor Day, we relented unwillingly to this part of life, and each Memorial Day, we threw off our burdens and headed down the Garden State Parkway for the first of many times during those three glorious months. Family friends all owned houses within the same five or six blocks in that tiny beach town, encamped in succession by other tiny beach towns, on that long, narrow barrier island we call the Jersey Shore.

The place is so much a part of me that when I went to live overseas temporarily, I brought a little Ziploc baggie full of sand from Harding Avenue in Ortley Beach. I wanted it with me. I wish I could have bottled up the air, too—the air that, with my first step out of the car upon arriving, I'd always inhale as much as my lungs could take.

This is delight: A white sun pushing through the blinds; Dad strolling in from the bakery with fresh rolls; the scent of sunscreen; Mom laying out rows of sandwiches to pack for the beach; kicking off my flip flops as soon as my feet hit the sand; toeing the ocean and the little gasp when I let the wave go through me; seawater drying in salty lines on my skin; a mouth stained with cherry Italian ice; the crunch of sand when I bit my cold cut sandwich; dozing off on my towel while John Sterling's voice announcing the Yankee game on the radio drifted in and out; fabric lines imprinted on my sleepy face; deep shadows in pockets of sand in late afternoon; stragglers throwing a frisbee on an emptying beach; the pink- and purple-stained clouds, the seagulls' tiny legs motoring along the edge of the surf; an outdoor shower under a soft sun; Uncle Tommy cleaning crabs over a bucket; our footsteps on the stones; the front porch picnic table; the passing of plates; the breeze.

When I became older and more introspective, the ocean was a place that invited contemplation. (Who doesn't feel wistful while looking at the ocean?) I inserted certain rituals into the day—like riding my bike to watch the sunset on the bay. I was pulled by longing to do these things, and did not feel fully myself, fully present, at the shore if I didn't do them. These rituals filled my soul's need to contemplate and wonder. I sensed my aliveness—as a creature sitting before a creator. I felt that such beauty happened on purpose, some sign of cosmic goodness displayed for me to enjoy. To this day, these scenes make me nostalgic for a home I don't quite remember but somehow deeply miss. The ocean is where I engage with mystical experience, and the gratitude, awe, longing, wrestling, and yearning that comes with it.

When Hurricane Sandy happened in 2012, the news teams called Ortley Beach "Ground Zero." The bay and the ocean had rushed to touch each other, the seawater gushing down the avenues, completely covering the skinny strip of land in muck and debris. My family watched the news in horror. One of the bridges to the mainland was sagging into the bay. The iconic Jet Star rollercoaster at the outer edge of the Seaside Pier sat twisted and ragged in the breaking waves amidst the remnants of wooden beams. The aerial camera panned over blocks of houses flattened or wiped away, when—*gasp!*—the corner lot at the end of Harding Avenue. Except, our house wasn't there, only the foundation— like a construction project abandoned in its early stages. The sound of muffled cries could be heard in the room as we stared at the TV: There we saw the dilapidated remains of our beloved vacation home, hovered over by a news channel helicopter, its blades casting a chopping shadow on the empty lot.

Restoring the Jersey Shore was slow; many FOR SALE signs went up, and some lots remain bare. Iconic portions of the boardwalk have become scenes of the past. Those that have been rebuilt don't feel quite the same. The pier doesn't stick out as far; the wood of the boardwalk has been replaced; there's a new roller-coaster called the Star Jet, but it's a different shape and color. Five years later, even the house is different—it's modern, new, and beautiful, but it feels foreign, at least for now. It is something to celebrate for sure, but it also feels like a new era, and a new era means the end of an old one. Memories are divided into before and after. We can still breathe in the salty air and hear the whistles and chimes of the arcades from our balcony; we can still sit on the beach until dusk and then BBQ in the stone yard; we can still walk the boards and consume waffles and ice cream. But some sight, sound, or smell inevitably arrives, reminding us it's not the same, evoking a sense of missing "the way it used to be."

Nostalgia has that mystifying effect on us; it's a longing for something we can't quite put our fingers on. But what if we could go back? What if we could somehow insert ourselves into the past? I suspect it wouldn't feel the same, anyway—because we are not the same as we were then.

It takes faith and patience to embrace the rebuilding of something that was lost. Patience because rebuilding is often slower than we would like it to be; faith because the new version may look different than it was before. And we have to choose to believe that the remake is its own good, that it will be greater than or equal to the one before. Will we rebuild? Yes. Will it be the same? No, but that's the point. House, boardwalks, arcades—what are they? But the ocean waves, the sky, the sunrises and sunsets—these remain the constant backdrop for our togetherness, reminding us to be nostalgic for something more eternal.

My Childhood Home
by Eileen Coughlin

She was the one with the green canvas
awning over beveled window glass.
The walls were Spanish lace stucco.
A teardrop crystal chandelier hung
at the center of a plaster fruit medallion
surrounded by hand-painted peaches
and clusters of purple grapes.

The dining room door swung
in double action into the kitchen.
An iron skillet sat on the stove
where the flank steak was seared.
There was a cozy breakfast nook near
a vintage wrought iron radiator—
warm, she was, to the touch.

2.
Boarded up on Wilshire, the east side
of the motor city, her burnt clay
body is buckling at the corners. Ivy
crawls through cracks in the cement

stairs. The green milk chute misses
its hinges—hanging—broken—empty
Abandoned. Nailed shut.

Gang symbols are scrawled
on the back of peeling plasterboard.
Tubs and toilets torn out.
The dusty lavender and black tile
around the bath of this former
brick beauty bulges. The weight
of decline more than she can bear.

3.

Condemned notices are pinned
to her rotting beams. Warning—
Stay out. She's dangerous. Her water
is shut off, electric lines cut,
gas clamped, inside stairs removed,
a rickety ramp without a railing
the only access to the upper floor.

Exposed.
Stripped.
Naked.
She is put up for auction
Sold in 2022
to the highest bidder
120 dollars.

Scudder Pond Through the Seasons
by Nancy Canyon

At the eastern entrance to Whatcom Falls Park, Scudder Pond shimmers, timeless in its filling and emptying, like a breathing entity, expanding, contracting, revealing, and concealing. The pond is a personality—opening and closing with the seasons.

In the early spring, chorus frogs are deafening. We can hear them a block away inside our house. The chorus chirps at dusk, starting and stopping, at first a quiet pianissimo but soon growing to a crescendo forte. There are other frogs in the pond as well. Harrumphing bullfrogs, for one, and another frog that screams like a girl when you step too close. I laugh every time I hear it.

Come spring, the pond becomes a yearly nesting place for mallards and geese, all fighting for the best hiding places in the reeds to lay eggs. One year, an inexperienced goose couple set up on a tiny island near the pond edge. When I passed, I said to the female, "I can see you!" I hoped the reeds would grow fast and hide the naïve twosome from predators. A short time later, the pair was gone, chased off by a more experienced goose couple.

Rain falls, and the greenery turns lush, cattails growing quickly, their velvety brown tops pristine, as do the lily pads, poking their diploma curls through the surface much earlier than I expect. The fresh, new leaves unfurl, their tender meatiness and spring green pads soon marred by beaver bites along yellow edges. The pads flatten out, and their arrow shapes turn the color of lilacs and sometimes a color I find hard to describe—both purple and brown and a tad orange at the same time. A color I rarely see in nature, a color that quickly changes to Irish green with bright yellow piping edging the leaves. Sun-drenched water glistens inside their boat shapes, inviting damsel and dragonflies to the lush mass. Additionally, diving ducks dabble in bottom mud close to the lilies, and occasionally goldeneyes forage the pond. Colorful wood duck couples fly in from their nest boxes tacked to nearby trees. Canada geese fly over, honk, land, and take off with splashes of exuberance. A rush of delight fills me.

The frog chorus ends around the time mosquitoes arrive. This is my least favorite time at Scudder Pond. I am always hurrying past the water to avoid the swarm, as they find my tender skin a pleasant feast. Though I love seeing the bats flying at dusk, swooping and diving, gulping down the juicy insects, I could do without mosquitoes entirely.

With warmer days, the pond slowly begins to dry up, and the swampy smell of mud predominates. Pond water is filtered by cattails, grasses, and yellow water lily, also known by a less flattering name—Spatterdock. Rhizomes connect to long stems and leaves. The rhizomes sometimes break the surface when the pond is low. Low water and a smell like mudflats at low tide are common. The tide is out in a way, as rains don't replenish the drink during the summer. The water grows so low mid-summer that rhizomes surface, their black twisty tubers looking like mythical water creatures. A great blue heron steps past the rhizomes, her slow-motion movement on sticklike legs barely disturbing the surface, her neck a loop and long beak a spear ready to snag a frog.

Bullfrogs harrumph, a sound like bulls bellowing that makes me chuckle. Sometimes they can be spotted sunning themselves on a log or rock alongside three big turtles resting near the reedy island hiding the beaver den. The waiting heron startles me with a quick strike. It takes several seconds for the bird to subdue and eat a bullfrog.

Seeing a beaver on land has never occurred for me, but the woodchips left behind by the big-toothed creature are proof of its presence. The beaver works hard at night, leaving behind huge piles of fresh chips at the base of felled trees. I have marveled at its stamina and brute strength, felling small alders near the pond overnight. Once, while walking past the pond, I was startled by a huge splash behind and off to my right, a sound like a boulder falling from the sky. I turned to the pond and watched ripples roll out from the epicenter. It was the beaver slapping the water with its tail. I didn't see it, but its warning shot was clear: *You don't belong here*, it seemed to say. *Move along.*

Summer is lush, replete with red-winged blackbirds, bumble and honeybees, berries, wild roses, dandelions, deadly nightshade, honey-suckle, morning glory, horsetail, nettles, and an occasional remaining mosquito, which I find more acceptable than a swarm. With warmer weather, a lavender layer of scum begins to cover the surface at the north end of the pond, a delicate fern-like organism that is said to help cleanse the water.

Crowds of people birdwatch, bicycle, push strollers, and run or walk the path. Dogs are prevalent. People stop and pick blackberries for cobblers or delicate thimbleberries to eat on the spot. Ocean Spray's drooping cream-colored flowers fill the woods with a sweet scent, Indian plum's fruit ripens, and yellow lily flowers open. Eagles sometimes fly low over the pond, and the call of the osprey high above leaves me with an eerie feeling. And, of course, deer enter and leave the path unexpectedly. The weather seems to change from summer to fall just like that. Suddenly, Scudder Pond comes alive with creativity and has the energy to redecorate. The lily pads turn speckled-yellow and brown, folding in on themselves, rocking with gusts of wind. Before a windstorm followed by heavy rain, lily pads thickly populated the pond's surface—now a crowd of tall stems, their heavy leaves crumpled like small paper bags, lean together. The color of brown paper describes them perfectly, and yes, there are still occasional green leaves or a yellow stem or two. But with the drizzling gray sky and the chill in the air, the pond is at its most ugly. I don't like using that word, as to me the withering lilies are still beautiful, dark and muted, what a painter might describe as a neutral color—the color arrived at when mixing complementary colors together.

The dark indigo sky is a striking backdrop to the orange leaves of the osier dogwoods and the yellowed leaves of the tattered cattails. Cattail heads bend sideways, fluff matted and pinched, escaping like stuffing from a torn cushion. The lily pads are mostly gone now. Alder leaves have dropped, scattering about with wind gusts.

Everything I love about the pond—the heart-shaped lily pads, red-winged blackbirds hopping across meaty leaves, lifting an edge to peck an insect from beneath, and the sky above reflecting on the surface—is complete for the year. The pond's surface is naked, bare stemmed, and leafless, the brown tops having blown away by 30 mph gusts, leaving the surface shining like black car glass that one cannot see through.

Along the edge of the pond, the gravel path meanders, finding dogwalkers and bird watchers sauntering past spent canary grass, wild roses with hips, native spirea, thimble and blackberries, red-osier dogwood, red-winged blackbirds, and small mammals. Serious birders carry binoculars and cameras and study the wildlife sanctuary for "life birds"—rare individuals that are not yet included on the birder's "life list"—hoping to spot one on this Great Washington State Birding Trail.

The deep woods beyond the pond shelter squirrels, raccoons, deer, chipmunks, shy birds hiding in the underbrush, and even, once, a mountain lion. River otters can sometimes be seen scrambling out of the water and crossing the path, scaring the mallards out of the pond to huddle on the bank. On the other side of the path, water rushes into the mixing area for lake water and cleansed runoff—the outlet for Lake Whatcom.

As the weather turns colder, a skim of ice forms at times in leafy crystals, first at the pond edge, feathery ice following the perimeter, delicate and easily broken, like the burnt sugar topping on crème brûlée. Later, when the season dives deeper into winter and all the leaves are gone, the bare brush edging the pond is decorated with snowberries, rose hips, dried blackberries, and Indian plum. If the temperatures drop further, the pond will freeze over with a sheet of ice that will hold my weight. If I am lucky, the ice will be flat and mirrored like the water when the weather is still. But if snow falls heavily atop the ice, thaws, and freezes again, it will be tooth-jarringly bumpy.

I will bring my skates when the ice is thick and smooth. I will feel like a young girl again when I tie them on and step out onto the ice, watching for cracks as my blades speed across the slick surface, bubbles moving beneath. Once, I saw a beaver swimming under the ice, bringing its face to the clear sheet, looking upward, darting away as the blades of my skates skimmed past. Another time, my dog walked out onto the ice and tried to get traction as I skated by—a cartoon dog, slip-sliding, scrambling to move forward but going nowhere. How I laughed at her that day!

But having a freeze that lasts long enough to thicken the ice so it will hold my weight has only happened twice in the twenty years I have lived in Bellingham. When I was young, I looked forward to winter and skating. The Spokane Parks Department flooded the parking lot at Audubon Park, and we waited for it to freeze. It wasn't beautiful like Scudder Pond, where the birds are fed by a steward who leaves piles of millet and black sunflower seed from the entrance to just past the pond's southern edge where forest abounds. Small birds eat the seed, as do mallards and squirrels. Even my dog is interested in snuffling the seed . . . what a treat!

As winter fades and deer and raccoon tracks melt, a waft of spring carries on the breeze. Cherry blossoms unfurl early. Green blackberries begin to form. Finally, the salmonberry flowers bloom, heralding the Swainson thrush and its melodious ascending warble. So beautiful!

Blue herons stand stick-still, waiting to spear frogs. Then there are the boisterous raccoons living around the pond who also hunt frogs. Once, I heard them fighting in the reeds. The sound of their snarling and growling reminded me of the mountain lion, but most claim they are mating . . . it's that time of year again.

Can you hear the frogs?

Ocean Snow
by Taya Sanderson Kesslau

It snows *in* the ocean.
From the surface of the water
all the way down to the floor.

White and fluffy flakes
each unique in form
composition.
Sand, soot
bits of phytoplankton.

It can take days and days
for a single particle
to drift to the seabeds below.

Imagine that—looking up
from the depths
into the space of eternity
waves of blues and greens
scattered light swallowed
in watery molecules.

An armored gilled-creature
at the bottom of the world
swaying in the deep currents
nourished and baptized
in the magical falling flurries

.

Life or Death on the Interstate
by Seán Thomas Dwyer

In winter, the five-hour drive from Grand Rapids, Michigan, to Mattoon, Illinois, could easily become an eight-hour slog on an icy interstate, which is dangerous as well as mind-numbing. But the past week had been sunny and cold, so the roads were as clear as in summertime, minus the road work. My drive to visit friends would be a breeze.

I left Michigan at 2:00 p.m. on a clear but frigid New Year's Eve afternoon in 1998. My girlfriend, Susan, and several of our friends awaited me in Mattoon for a small gathering that would carry over to 1999. Mattoon was a sleepy town of 64,000 White people just off Interstate 57. Best known for producing Lender's Bagels and home to the original Burger King, this thriving metropolis was where I would party like it was 1999, until it suddenly *was* 1999.

I blazed through Indiana and past Chicago in my very used Acura Integra, the only car I could afford in my first year as a full-time college instructor. It had a four-speed manual transmission that tended to pop out of fourth gear at inopportune times, and the gas gauge was accurate from full to half-full, at which point the needle always decided I didn't need to know its business and thus left me with a false sense of security.

I stopped every hundred miles to fill the tank because it was below zero across most of the Midwest, and I didn't have AAA to bail me out. I had no cell phone, for that matter, because I had heard of them but knew no one who owned one. It was just me and the highway and my tunes, which consisted of whatever country station came into range after I left Chicago's WOJO behind.

On my way south, I passed towns whose names I knew from news reports on WGN-AM in Chicago: Monee, Beecher, Peotone, Grant Park, and Bourbonnais. Bourbonnais was where my bubble burst. Rather, that was where one of my tires exploded.

When I bought the Acura for $700 from a guy who told me he had recently put retread tires on it, I had no idea that the new tread, applied to old sidewalls, was like putting new wine into old wineskins. I found out when, well after dark and while "There's Your Trouble" by the Dixie Chicks was spilling out of my speakers, I heard a bang and found myself fighting the Acura to keep it between the lines.

The good aspect of having this tire blow in north-central Illinois on New Year's Eve was that no traffic had to swerve to avoid me. This isolation was also the terrible aspect of the tire's timing. As I rolled to a stop, the DJ announced a temperature of fifteen degrees before spinning "No Place That Far."

First-aid training says the first step is to "assess the situation." I learned the same thing in the Boy Scouts. I started assessing my butt off.

I exited the car and saw that the passenger's rear tire had left the tread far behind. I could not roll on the flat tire because there was no tire. I looked ahead and saw bright lights on the opposite

side of the freeway, at least a mile away. Out here, it had to be a
gas station.

Didn't it?

I scurried back into the car, the southeasterly wind trying to
wrest the door from my hands. I was not on a day trip, so I had
clothes I could layer to run to the light if it came to that. I turned
the heater on high and sat back. I lit my flashers, and every time
a trucker drove by, I flicked my headlights in Morse code. Surely
one good buddy would call in my distress signal to the Illinois
State Police.

Wouldn't he?

I checked my fuel gauge. The needle sat at a comforting half
tank. Or should I feel comforted? I realized I had been looking
for a gas station for a while already because I had hit the half-tank
plateau just south of Chicago. I could turn the car off and restart
it when I began to feel a chill. That would save gas until my Good
Samaritan rolled up.

I turned off the car, and the flashers turned off. Oh, yes, that
was an Acura feature: no flashers without accessory power. I
couldn't turn the ignition to the accessory position without risking
a dead battery later. My car was an invisible rectangle, far too close
to the white line should a Drunk Samaritan head in my direction.

Untenable was the descriptor that popped into my mind when
I further assessed my plight. I was not one to carry a sleeping bag
and a Thermos of coffee in my hatchback, and since my hosts
paid their utility bills, I expected not to have to bundle up in their
house. I had my winter coat and gloves, but I had donned my
tennis shoes with no thought to a late-night excursion in the
brutal cold.

I started the engine again and again over the next hour, and
then I felt the gut-punch understanding that no truckers or

troopers would be helping me. I turned and looked through my overnight bag to see what warm clothing I had brought as a change for New Year's Day. I had an undershirt I could pull over the one I was wearing and a sweater I could button over my pullover. I yanked off my sweater, and the shock of the cold struck me. Second undershirt in place, I hurried into my sweater and added the cardigan. Finally, I prepared to pull on my parka, but first, there was the question of my pants.

I was wearing jeans, but I had a pair of thick corduroys that would serve me better. It was one or the other; I had not brought long johns or sweats. Shoes off, jeans off, legs freeze, chilly cords on, blast heat until warm, stick feet up to heater vent, replace shoes, apply parka and gloves, turn off car, and sprint out the door into a bitter headwind.

The real irony here would have been if I had stepped into the path of the only car to pass in the past hour, but the lanes were as empty as the vacuum of space. I ran across the two lanes, which are broader than one realizes, then into the long, frosty grass heading down to a dip between the northbound and southbound lanes. At the far white line of the northbound lanes, I turned and dashed south. My first milestone would be to reach an overpass that now blocked the lights from my view. After that, I should be able to tell if the lights were a gas station or a commercial building I would have to break into.

I was a mile into my run and getting winded when I learned, to my relief, that the main light ahead was a welcoming Phillips 66 sign. I slowed to a trot for a bit to catch my breath, but I never walked. The wind, slamming into my face, tried pushing me off the shoulder and onto the freeway lane. After ten steps, I resumed my pace, with just another mile to go.

My upper body, head, and hands were warm still when the wind started seeping into my pants. *Thud, thud, thud,* went my feet, but I realized I could not lift them as high, nor stride as far, as when I started my jaunt. It wasn't from poor conditioning. My thighs were freezing up. With a half mile to go, I started staggering like a zombie. I pounded my thighs with my fists to wake them up. No luck.

Go to the light, I heard myself thinking. The line from *Toy Story* held a sinister undertone I found unnerving. Leaden step after leaden step, I pushed forward, vowing to crawl if it came to that, and dragging my legs if rigor set in. One hundred yards. *Like one hundred years of solitude.* Memories of cross-country races in junior high streamed through my mind, the last half mile always full of stumbles and chest cramps. If I tripped or cramped up here, I would die. In "To Build a Fire," the character's death didn't seem painful. That was some consolation in this predicament. But I wanted to watch the ball drop at Susan's house. So, on I plodded. Not even beating my thighs kept the muscles moving now. I moved forward by swiveling my hips.

And then, I don't know how, I reached the berm of the parking lot and used my hands to lift my legs onto the pavement. I crossed frozen asphalt, a few inches at a time. The light was bright enough near the building for someone to notice me before I died. But there were no cars at the pumps. With traffic this slow, would they have closed for the holiday?

If so, I would have to bust in. An alarm would be a welcome sound. I pulled my leg onto the step up to the door and yanked on the handle. It opened.

A bearded man stood at the register, yakking it up with a guy in flannel and a blaze-orange cap. They turned to me when I leaned against an end cap and gasped with relief. "Can I use the phone? My car's dead a couple of miles north of here."

Orange Cap's jaw dropped. "Holy crap," he exclaimed as he pointed to the far door. I limped past the grocery aisles to the phone and yanked off my right glove. I dialed my friend Susan's number in Mattoon, which seemed a universe away. When the robot operator requested a dollar, I pulled a handful of icy coins from my pants pocket. I dropped four quarters into the coin slot, and the *boops* and *beeps* and two rings connected me to Susan.

She sounded relieved that I was safe, but I heard some judgment in her tone. "You didn't dress for the weather? You don't have the best car."

"Right now, I have the worst possible car. I'll have to hang out here until morning unless I can get a tow tonight."

"Don't do that. I'll call Ed and Patty and have them come for you." I had forgotten that I was just miles from Susan's sister and brother-in-law in Bourbonnais. They knew me from an Easter dinner Susan had invited me to, so there would be no hesitation in rescuing me. "Can you get tires in the morning?"

I did the mental math. I had enough for two tires in my checking account. I admitted that, and Susan said, "Hmm. Don't tell Ed why you're only getting two tires. It's kind of awkward."

Ed was the fire chief in Bourbonnais. If I had called 911, he might well have been the responder anyway. When I turned from the phone, Orange Cap held out a Styrofoam cup of coffee. "On us," he said, nodding in the direction of the cashier. "Need any food?"

I walked over to the heat lamp that was keeping the hot dogs warm. After I thawed my hands under the red glow, I tonged a hot dog and nestled it in a warm bun. I shuffled toward the cashier, but he waved me off.

Ed reached the 66 quicker than I expected, but then, he generally had to drive fast as part of his job. By the time he pulled up in his Buick, I could walk normally again. When he walked through the door, tall and muscular, with a thick mustache keeping his mouth warm, I almost collapsed with relief.

He drove me to my car to get my bag and arranged a tow to his preferred tire dealer. We waited in Ed's toasty car while the tow-truck operator hoisted my forlorn Acura, and once my car was on its way, Ed and I raced to his house. Patty, Susan's lookalike blonde, blue-eyed sister, made soothing sounds, settled me into a recliner, and put a comforter over my legs. She offered me some chicken noodle soup, and as the broth and noodles warmed my belly, I started to shake from relief at having survived this mess.

Ed flicked on the TV, where a 1998 retrospective was playing, currently focusing on Frank Sinatra's life, which had ended in May. He and I chatted about his role in keeping the town safe; he asked me if I changed my smoke-detector batteries at every time change. I assured him that I did. Patty asked how my new teaching job was going. I said it was enjoyable, but I didn't mention that the pay was crap. That would be obvious in the morning, when I would retain the best two retreads and buy two new tires.

We all were asleep before midnight. I didn't know if they generally stayed up for the ball to drop but this year I had stressed them out too much, or if they just didn't bother. Down in Mattoon, Susan was still hosting a small gathering. I would get to see her on the first.

Ed and I rose early to get to the tire dealer. In addition to the major miracle of my surviving the run to the 66 station, it was a minor miracle that the shop opened on New Year's Day and didn't cost me the chagrin of mooching another night at Ed and Patty's house.

Susan was right about Ed; he looked startled when I bought just two tires. "I'll get the other two after I transfer money out of savings to cover them," I explained. My embarrassment almost made me wish I had been found in my car in the morning, an oblivious popsicle.

Ed drove us back to the house, where Patty served us a robust Midwestern breakfast. My profuse thanks for their help seemed inadequate, but I figured I would ask Susan about an appropriate gift when I saw her.

With my belly full, I bade Patty goodbye, and Ed reunited me with my car. I filled my gas tank at the closest station, because I didn't trust the gauge enough to be sure I'd make it to the 66 to give them my money. I waved at the 66 as I passed it, wishing that business well.

After I visited Susan, I made it back to Grand Rapids intact, and the first thing I did was toss a sleeping bag and thermal underwear in the hatchback. My next paycheck covered two more tires, and I finally felt whole again, capable of withstanding a Michigan winter.

Where I Come From . . .
by Ron Ruthruff

17,000 dollars can buy you
A brand-new home
Avocado shag carpets
Single car garage
Three bedrooms, one bath
You just gotta become an American citizen.

I am from Petty Coat Junction
Mayberry
Small town, two lights
Bum Fuck No Where

Taco Flats
That's what "they" called us
Victor, Alex, Benito, Billy
But we are all Taco Flats
A little leaven leavens the whole loaf

Ronnie, if you know me
Who's that ONE-EYED KID? if ya don't
Cyclopes
Pirate
One eye's gonna be none eye

I am from a place of one visit to the doctor's office
White walls
Orange chairs

A little boy waits for his father
But goes home with only his Mother
A little boy sits home alone
No one sits at the kitchen table
TV dinners
TV trays
TV guides
TV guides my life

I am from a place where an old woman
Gets a job for one dollar and sixty cents per hour
A Certified Nurse's Aide buys her boy a color TV
Pastors buy big houses
Widows pay big tithes

Where is your dad?
Why is your mom so old?
Why is your mom so FAT?
Why do you wear the same pair of jeans every day?
Where did you get your sneakers?
What's wrong with your eye?

I am from a place where I still hear my teachers
Rebellious
Incorrigible
Curr
Greaser
Reptile Ronnie
Sticks and stones may break my bones
But names, they shape me

A Single mom teaches her son to love
Empty a bedpan
Wipe an eighty-year-old Ass
Shave a dead man
That's how you love for a buck sixty an hour

You see, I am from a place
Where what your daddy does is who you are
But I am from my Mother

Utopia
by Marian Exall

To Mrs Elmhirst Claridges Hotel London Stop Come Totnes Soonest Stop Found Perfect Place Stop Leonard.

The terse wording of the telegram managed to convey Leonard Elmhirst's excitement as well as his Yorkshire carefulness with money. His new wife, Dorothy née Whitney, had grown up surrounded by Gilded Age wealth in New York. She waved the flimsy yellow form with irritation.

"Hilary! Where on earth is Tot . . . ens? Why can't he use the telephone like a normal person?"

Hilary James occupied an ambiguous position in the Elmhirst household, somewhere between companion, secretary, and lady's maid. A vicar's daughter with a good education, she had lost her husband in the final year of the Great War. Introduced to the Elmhirsts by a friend of her father, she had drifted into this job as she had drifted through everything since her husband's death. She took the telegram from Dorothy.

"Totnes is in Devon, I believe." She pronounced the place name correctly, the accent on the second syllable. "It's quite rural. There may not be many telephones there."

Dorothy made a dismissive sound. "Do they have a railroad station at least? You'd better see about getting us tickets. And pack a bag for me—nothing fancy. If they don't have telephones, I doubt we'll be dressing for dinner."

Twenty-four hours later, Dorothy and Hilary alighted at Totnes station. Hilary secured a porter to manage the luggage while the newlyweds reunited with a kiss that made other travelers stare. Although Hilary suspected Dorothy's avowed democratic ideals cloaked a stubborn sense of moneyed entitlement, she never doubted her employers' love for each other. Dorothy, too, had lost a husband. Willard Straight, another scion of a wealthy New York family, had died of influenza in 1918, leaving Dorothy with three young children. She turned to philanthropy, determined to put her substantial fortune to worthy use in the aftermath of world war and global pandemic. Leonard was six years her junior and shared her idealism. Having studied in India with Tagore, a Bengali poet, philosopher, and social reformer, he'd convinced Dorothy that they should establish a utopian community in England, a grand experiment with artists, farmers, educators, and writers working and living together. He had driven away from London the week before with a list of possible sites, one in Devon.

"Dartington Hall was built in the fourteenth century. The original family died out a hundred years ago, and the estate fell into disrepair. The current owner lives in Australia and leases the land to local farmers," Leonard explained over his shoulder as the three motored away from the station.

"Is anyone living in the Hall now?" asked Dorothy.

"Well, no . . . As I said, the place needs work."

In the dusk, approached by an avenue of ancient oak trees, the gatehouse looked romantic: grey stone and mullioned windows.

Hilary noted the absence of glass in those windows. They left the car and proceeded on foot under the arch toward the main house.

"Watch out!" Leonard grabbed Dorothy's arm as she was about to step into a cowpat. The inner courtyard was a rough pasture, dotted with wildflowers and the malodorous evidence of cattle. The Hall ahead of them was in ruins, roof beams poking above the walls. Crows wheeled and screeched around the crenellated battlements, lending an air of gothic mystery. Hilary thought of the generations that once lived here, the snorts of warhorses, the smell of cooking fires, the ring of hammer on anvil. All long silent.

"What's he doing?" Dorothy's voice was faint as she pointed to a man and a dog herding cows toward the building.

"I think he's putting the cows in for the night," Hilary speculated.

"In the Hall? Leonard, we need to talk."

Hilary left the couple to reconcile their visions for the grand experiment. Raised in the countryside, she was not afraid of cows. She walked through the high grass toward the man, grateful for her stout shoes.

"Good evening, sir. Do you mind if I have a look inside?"

The cowman had a ruddy face and sun-bleached hair. He was younger than Hilary first thought. One empty sleeve of his canvas jacket was pinned across his chest; he'd served at the Front, she guessed. He gestured with his remaining hand.

"Ye're welcome to look, but be careful. The stairs aren't sound." His voice had a soft Devon burr. "Let me get these creatures to bed, and I'll give ye a tour."

She glanced back to see Dorothy and Leonard's heads together in conversation. "All right." While she waited, she surveyed the walls of the building. The battlements were intact, as were the soaring stone frames of the window apertures. Yes, part of the roof had collapsed, but she could see the possibilities for restoring the Hall to livable space.

"I'm Steven Shottery. I won't shake hands as I've been with the herd." His smile was friendly, and Hilary got the impression of a confident man at ease with life.

"My name's Hilary James. I'm with . . ." she indicated the Elmhirsts, "I think they may be interested in purchasing the place."

Steven laughed. "Well, good luck to 'em. It'll take some work, but I think the old house is worth it."

"What about your cows?" Hilary bent to scratch behind the herding dog's ears, also to avoid the man's gaze. His direct manner flustered her. She couldn't remember the last time she'd been alone with an attractive man—not since Jeremy was killed.

"Oh, there's other spaces I can put 'em. The estate's hundreds of acres. They'll not want to tackle all of it at once." He looked at Leonard and Dorothy, approaching over the grass.

"Leonard's an agronomist, interested in modern farming methods. I think he'll want to work with local farmers to develop the estate," Hilary said in a rush, wanting to find common ground to ease an introduction between the men.

Indeed, Leonard was eager to talk about his ideas with Steven, one countryman to another, leaving Hilary and Dorothy to wander around the Hall and the other smaller structures— stables?—on either side of the pasture. These too were in a tumbledown state, but they might be repurposed as studios for artisans attracted to the project, a space for concerts and dance recitals, classrooms for a progressive school for the children.

Leonard had clearly succeeded in overcoming Dorothy's initial unfavorable impression, which was essential as Dorothy would be providing the funds for this quixotic adventure.

The next morning when she came down to breakfast from her room at the country inn where they were staying, Hilary felt a shock of pleasure at seeing Steven Shottery in the entrance hall. She'd been thinking about him. Today, he had swapped farmer's garb for a tweed suit.

"How on earth did you find me?" she asked, then put a hand over her mouth as if to push the involuntary words back in.

Steven grinned. "And good morning to you, Miss James. As the Cott Inn's the only decent lodging within miles, 'twas a safe guess. Tell the truth, Mr. Elmhirst invited me to meet him here before we tour the estate."

At that moment, Leonard came down the stairs, hand extended. "Mr. Shottery, I'm looking forward to this!" Then he turned to Hilary. "Won't you join us for breakfast, Hilary? Dorothy's taking hers in the room and then writing to the children. She won't need you, and I'm sure Mr. Shottery won't object."

Steven and Hilary followed Leonard into the dining room. While they devoured eggs and homemade sausage, washed down by surprisingly good coffee, the men discussed optimum herd size and the merits of Jerseys versus Fresians. Leonard described the farming experiments he'd seen in the United States and his plans for introducing them at Dartington. Hilary was silent, making mental notes to relay to Dorothy. Although she was more interested in the cultural aspects of their utopian experiment, Dorothy wanted to be kept abreast of every project—after all, she was paying.

While Leonard went to get the car, Hilary and Steven said goodbye at the entrance.

"I hope we'll meet again, Miss James."

"It's missus, not miss—I'm a widow." Unnecessary details. "And I do, too. I mean . . ." Her words stuttered to silence, and she was grateful for Leonard's toot on the horn as he drew up outside. Steven bowed and turned away, saying over his shoulder, "Please call me Steven. May I call you Hilary?" She nodded, feeling her cheeks redden.

The next two weeks were filled with activity. Terms were agreed upon with the absentee owner for the purchase of the Dartington estate, a suitable house was located for the Elmhirsts to occupy while renovations took place at the Hall, and passage was booked for Dorothy to return to New York to prepare her children for their new life in Devon.

"I don't know why you won't come," Dorothy complained to Hilary. "You'd have an opportunity to see New York, and we'll be back here in a month."

"I'll be more use here. I can get the house ready for the family, hire staff, write letters, and keep the accounts for Leonard—"

"I suppose so. Just don't go running off with some handsome farmer—we need you!"

In fact, Hilary only saw Steven in the distance or in passing. She had time for little else than following Leonard's whirlwind directions, which were interspersed with his animated explanation of the theories underpinning the project.

"It would be easier if you knew how to drive," Leonard sighed. "I don't want to take time away from the site, but there are errands to run to the lawyers in Exeter, and the architect in Kingsbridge. I'll ask Steven to teach you." Hilary didn't mention that she had driven her father on pastoral visits before she was married.

When Leonard made the request to Steven, he laughed. "I haven't driven a motor since I lost my arm, but I think I remember how. I've time before afternoon milking. Would you like to make a start now, Mrs. James?"

Before Hilary could reply, Leonard interjected. "Excellent! Can you run these letters to the post office?"

"You've done this before, haven't you?" Steven commented as they drew up outside the grocery shop in Totnes, which also served as a post office. Although Leonard's Daimler Tourer was larger and more powerful than her father's Austin, Hilary managed the clutch and throttle without stalling and only crashed the gears once.

"Yes," she admitted. "But I'm out of practice."

"Well then, we should go for a spin—get you used to these narrow lanes." He looked pleased at the prospect.

With minimal instruction, he guided her along country roads where they met little traffic. They stopped where a lane ended on a grassy headland overlooking the sea.

It seemed natural to take his hand as he led the way down a steep trail to the beach. Children were throwing pebbles into the water, their dog dashing into the waves in a fruitless attempt to retrieve them. Steven and Hilary stood watching.

"Did your husband die in France?" Steven asked.

Hilary nodded. "August 1918, Amiens. Where were you wounded?"

"1916, Battle of the Somme—the first one. All that for half a mile of ground." His voice was flat. "What do you make of this . . . utopian experiment?" The wry smile was back.

She shrugged. "I want to believe in a better world, but honestly? I think the Elmhirsts are naïve. Building the "new society" on a country estate? It's a childish dream."

"What do you dream of?"

Suddenly, she was crying, unable to speak. No one had asked about her dreams since the war. Family and friends tiptoed around her, perhaps in fear of an emotional outburst like this one.

Steven wrapped his one arm around her, holding her close and absorbing the sobs into his shoulder. "I'm sorry," he whispered.

She pulled away, searching for a handkerchief to wipe her face. "Forgive me. I don't usually break down like that. I try not to think of the war . . ." She turned her head, embarrassed.

Steven waited until he was sure she had control of her emotions. "We're all carrying losses. My older brother was killed, and my dad died of a broken heart. We think we're protecting ourselves by hiding our feelings, but perhaps we're just keeping the feelings prisoner. Maybe dreams are a way to set them free."

She looked back at him, but his gaze was roving over the headland, the sea, the children playing. "How do you manage . . . after all that?"

"I take comfort in this place, the beauty, the good rich soil . . . my cows." His eyes found hers, challenging her to smile.

"I was wrong to call the Elmhirsts naïve. They've suffered too. Leonard lost two brothers in the war, and Dorothy's first husband died of Spanish flu. It's just that their enthusiasm can be tiring."

He caught her hand. "Not too tired to drive, I hope?"

They spoke little on the way back. Her tears on the beach had taken away any reserve she once felt, but she appreciated his respect for her silence. After she parked at the gatehouse and Steven climbed out, he turned back with a frown. "I think you need more lessons before you're ready for the open road. That Daimler gearbox is tricky. Same time tomorrow?"

She matched his serious look. "Certainly, if you think it's necessary. I don't want to cause an accident." They broke into grins, which they struggled to contain as Leonard appeared waving a telegram.

"Dorothy's arriving in a week with the children! Now we can really get started!"

Leonard was oblivious to the burgeoning relationship between Steven and Hilary, but when Dorothy returned to Devon, she appraised the situation correctly.

"My dear, you are positively glowing! It's that handsome farmer Shottery, isn't it?" Dorothy held up a hand before Hilary could speak. "Don't deny it. At least he won't spirit you away from Dartington. Leonard has plans to develop a model dairy farm with that young man in charge—all the modern methods. And I have my own plans for you." She closed her eyes and pointed to an imaginary sign. "Dartington Dairy: finest cheeses, butter, and cream. Hilary James, proprietor."

"But I don't know anything about—" Hilary protested.

"You'll learn. We'll all learn. It's a grand utopian experiment!"

Author's Note: In 1925, Dorothy and Leonard Elmhirst purchased the neglected Dartington estate. They established the "Dartington Experiment": www.dartington.org/about/our-history/. Hilary and Steven are entirely fictional characters.

My Heart Tells Me
by Betty Scott

I.

Nick's silver truck pulls away, carrying a half-century of growth
and debris.

He wears heavy-duty coveralls, stiff from use, thick yellow
gloves, and goggles.

With a roar, he saws through and hauls the prickly limbs of two
Bird Nest Spruce

Home to moths, wasps, hornets, and a hideaway for raccoons!

He wears heavy-duty coveralls, stiff from use, thick yellow
gloves and goggles.

These spruce narrowed the walkway to my front door.

Home to moths, wasps, hornets, and a hideaway for raccoons!

He drags heavy limbs, lifts and throws them to the top of his
silver trailer.

These spruce narrowed the walkway to my front door.

A Deadly Night Shade is uprooted too.

He drags heavy limbs, lifts and throws them to the top of his
silver trailer.

Mesmerized, I stand at my window and watch the parade.

A Deadly Night Shade is uprooted too.
With a roar, he saws through and hauls the prickly limbs of two
  Bird Nest Spruce.
Mesmerized, I stand at my window and watch the parade.
Nick's silver truck pulls away, carrying a half-century of growth
  and debris.

II.

My heart tells me I need to be patient and loving.
Decode and decide what to keep, give to others, or throw out.
What will my children and grandchildren remember when I'm
  gone?
What legacy will I leave my friends and family?

Decode and decide what to keep, give to others, or throw out.
Shopping for food to cook at home is my craft.
What legacy will I leave my friends and family?
All the while, electricity tingles up and down my legs to my toes.

Shopping for food to cook at home is my craft.
Poetry aplenty is never enough.
All the while, electricity tingles up and down my legs to my toes.
There's always more I could and would do.

Poetry aplenty is never enough.
What will my children and grandchildren remember when I'm
  gone?
There's always more I could and would do.
My heart tells me I need to be patient and loving.

Pressing Apple Cider
by M'Lyn Avera

Sunlight filtered in from the broken window, highlighting Diane's gray hair. Her smile lifted her cheeks and increased the lines that fanned out from the corners of her eyes. Just a whisper of autumn caught in the air, and the sky was almost cloudless on that September morning. I was in my early twenties and rented the house next door to my landlord, Mary, on Baird Road in McKinleyville, California. Diane lived on the other side of the street. They had asked if I wanted to help press apple cider. The dilapidated shack that housed the vintage Italian press stood behind a small apple orchard. Wooden crates of apples were haphazardly placed along a metal fence overgrown with blackberries. Between the shack and crates were two large wine barrels filled with water and apples.

Mary stepped up onto a stool next to the shack and opened the twelve-by-twelve-inch door that gave access to a metal trough. She told me the apples would roll down into the pulverizing blades, and all I had to do was keep them coming. Mary flipped her long straight brown hair off her shoulder as she stepped down. She continued to explain how the process worked with clarity and patience.

"Are you ready?" Mary asked.

She flipped on the switch to the diesel generator, causing it to cough and sputter to life. I scooped up apples with her young daughter's purple plastic bucket and filled the trough. About twenty minutes later, the rhythmic sound of the engine came to a stop, and they asked me to join them inside the shack. The fruity sweet smell of apple juice and aged wood permeated the room. Under the iron wheel of the screw press were five burlap lined frames full of apple pulp. Mary and Diane stood on the base of the press, ready to crank it down, and extract the juice from the pulp.

"All you need to do is cap the jar with the lid and slide a new one under the spout until the flow stops," Mary instructed.

I looked at the mismatched assortment of glass bottles, gallon masons and large pickle jars. I grabbed one, twisted off the lid, and placed it under the spout. The juice started flowing, and so did the conversation. Mary and Diane talked about which manure made the best fertilizer. They discussed chicken and cow shit like my friends and I used to debate fashion and music. Not once were physical appearances mentioned. They were concerned with living life, the day-to-day chores, raising children, how much fruit their orchards had produced, and the process of milking goats and making goat cheese.

When the stream of juice became a trickle, they turned the screw press in the other direction, releasing the pressure and making room to pull out the trays. We emptied the apple pulp from the frames into a wheelbarrow parked outside the door. Once it was full, the contents were dumped onto the compost pile, and the process started all over again. We switched positions, and I folded the burlap cloth over the bulging pulp as the apple spray fell around me. Within a few hours, my hair became a sticky tangle of curls, and my jeans could have stood on their own.

These two women moved through the day with such confidence; I was in awe. Their hardy laughter bubbled up from a deep place, one filled from experiencing life fully. They laughed over situations and missteps that would irritate me or cause self-doubt. Their ability to learn from their mistakes and be done with them was like opening the windows in spring, refreshing. I wanted to ask them how they were able to move on with such grace but didn't. I tucked their laughter away in my mind so I could pull it out the next time I made a mistake, hoping to be a little gentler with myself.

We made over twenty gallons of apple cider that day. The crates by the fence were empty, and the compost piled high. After we lined up the filled jars and bottles along the side of the shack, we plopped down at the old cable spool table. When I folded my arms, they stuck together. Pulling them apart was like releasing a sticky jar of honey. Laughter broke out again, my laughter reaching down into my belly. Mary pulled herself up from the table and returned with the hose and a stack of towels. She rinsed off and turned the hose on the two of us. We played in the water like children on a hot summer day, giggling and dancing in uninhibited joy.

We dried off, put our hair up in towels, and wrapped dry ones around our shoulders. Diane suggested we open one of the bottles of apple cider and picked one from the end of the line. Mary walked into the house and came back with three glasses filled with ice cubes and a handful of raisins. I poured the apple cider we had just made into the glasses. Then we lifted them with a clink and drank what I named the nectar of McKinleyville goddesses. I included myself in that description and chuckled.

Sitting with our feet up, sipping fresh apple cider, we agreed we deserved a break after putting in a full day's work.

"What are the raisins for?" I asked.

Mary and Diane exchanged a coded smile that only happens among friends who have spent a lot of time together.

"Hard cider. We've perfected it over the years," Mary said. Diane explained that it takes about three weeks for fresh pressed to become hard cider and invited me to share a glass with them when it was ready.

I had just moved from Southern California to Humboldt County to attend the University, more for the redwood trees than the courses offered. McKinleyville had a traffic light or two on the main road and, to me, was a postcard-perfect image of rural living. The connection to these two women resonated in a way I had not known before. My friends and I hung out, went for hikes or to the movies together, but this was different. Without knowing it, without pushing an agenda, Mary and Diane had offered a window into community and how leaning on others isn't a sign of weakness. It just makes lighter work. These thoughts meandered through my mind with the slowing pace of the day.

Mary looked at me and smiled. "You look happy."

"I am. This apple cider is the best I have ever had. It feels good knowing we made it," I said.

We poured half a glass more, and Mary warned me not to drink too much or I would be in the bathroom all night. That comment sent us into another bout of laughter. When the laughter calmed down, Mary asked me if I wanted to learn how to milk goats. She said it would be helpful to have someone she could count on to milk them if she needed to be out of town. She milked her herd of twelve goats in the morning and again in the evening, which took roughly an hour each. She wanted to extend her goat milk production so she could sell more cheese, but explained with a shrug of her shoulder, there are only so many hours in a day.

"Once you learn how to milk them, if you want to take over a shift, we can trade for rent," she suggested.

"Yes, I'll do it!"

They both raised their glasses. Diane said, "That *yes* attitude will take you far. What do you want to do when you finish school?"

"I'm not sure, maybe travel. I love the visual arts, music, writing, and now cider making, but don't know if I can support myself."

"Making money is important, but enjoying what you do is important also. You know the Beatles' song 'Can't Buy Me Love'—I think that goes for happiness too," Diane said.

Mary chimed in, "There is something about doing what you love. I wanted a farm, and even though it's a lot of work, I am content, and even happy. Follow your heart, it will never steer you wrong."

I looked at them and wanted their words to be true. Mary was fearless and creative, with all kinds of projects going on at the same time. She put a new roof on the sheep's pen, made bee's wax candles, and sewed Halloween costumes for her girls. She was always busy but never seemed to be rushed. It was clear that following her heart made for a happy life.

The next week, we began my training. She took me into the converted garage which housed the pens and a milking station. The yellow and red begonias in hanging baskets on the side of the building were almost spent. Hay covered the floor, and a brass swinging lamp shone light onto the area. It took a bit of adjustment to apply the right amount of pressure to the goat's teats. A few days into milking on my own, one of the goats waited until I filled the pail with milk before kicking it over. Soon, I was milking the goats in the evenings and stashing my rent money away for the future. Milking the goats afforded me time with my thoughts. I often worked out problems or wrote papers in my mind while milking. I grew fond of the goats and their different personalities.

I am now the age Diane was that day forty years ago on Baird Road. Teaching became my passion, a place where sharing art processes and literature lit up my elementary students' imaginations. Working in ceramics with my hands in the clay or drawing and painting are avenues for self-expression that often reflect my close relationship with nature, especially the forests. Later, I became my mother's caregiver, where I found my inner strength and capacity to love.

Today, I walk the off-leash trail behind Lake Padden in Bellingham, Washington. Sunlight catches the yellow maple leaves that are still hanging on the trees, illuminating them against the dark green boughs of the conifers. I inhale deeply, taking in the autumn colors. The image of odd-sized jars lined up next to the shack and filled with apple cider wraps around me like a fleece robe in winter. Mary and Diane's vivid smiles glow like those jars. The memory of our friendship rekindles, warming their place in my heart like the amber color when the afternoon light filters through the hue of sweet apple cider.

Clayton Beach
by Tyson Higel

Out past the Groovy Douglas and Madrona trees,
past the plant whose name I can't remember
with toilet paper leaves, past the nurse stumps,
and railroad tracks, and sidetrack trails to who-knows-where,
lies a beach.

And at that beach, if you take a right, are rock formations,
with holes in them, that make sounds are good for climbing.
And the smaller rocks, the pebbles, the shells, all come
to meet the tide. Under the water are nudibranch and kelp
and all kind of fish—some that breach the water so high
you're jolted with excitement, something primitive.

Let us not forget the seal, who lives underneath as well,
who pops their head up out of water, looks, bobs with
the Salish, then dips under from here to there.
Swims thirty-three feet . . . forty feet . . . it's hard to tell.

What's easy is the calm of just being, of observation.
That special communal feeling of touching the water,
touching our roots. The same cells in different form
that are living, breathing, enjoying this magical creation.
The natural world, evolving always—me, and them, and you.

Three Bodies of Water: Orcas Island
by Ellen Graham

Cascade Lake

For reasons I don't quite understand, in June, I need to sit and watch Cascade Lake wake up.

Foxglove and monkey flower and one lone red poppy. Breeze and wind and whispers of wind and barely wind and insect wing wind. Goose poop. Still and hushed and breath holding. Low fog covers the lake. Crows and eagles and towhees and thrush. Sun peeping and warmth and daylight. No humans. The first laps of water. A pause.

Then one blue Ford bumping down the road, radio radio radio. Tires slapping.

An adolescent raven yelling *What? What? What?* Candy-colored kayaks (lime! cherry! lemon!). A backpack and a bandanna and bare feet. Early morning arrivals to get the best picnic table. One family, one blanket, one cooler, then two then three then four. *Thunk* of groceries on the picnic tables. *Chit chit* of chickadees looking for scraps. Tables covered with soot and juice and beer. Dogs, suddenly, two then three then a pack—barking, throwing their furry selves into the water! Smack! The whir of a

Frisbee. More cars, more doors slamming, more radio. Adolescent boys screaming *What? What? What?* Cigarettes dangling from their cherry mouths. Babies staggering like drunks into the shallows. Bleached towels, banana ice cream, and coffee. The promise of summer. June.

The Salish Sea

We are smelly and we are sweaty and we are happy. We have arrived at North Beach Cottages high above the Salish Sea. Our annual visit after three days of camping in Moran Park.

The Eagles Nest cottage is a tiny studio. And, yes, there are many eagles. An eagle carved into the fireplace, an eagle lamp, an eagle rug, and an eagle placemat. A carved wooden eagle outside. Eagle mugs and coasters, eagle salt and pepper shakers, eagle teapots and eagle tea containers. And yet completely charming.

There are rituals. I take out my red hots and my red tissue paper and my red candle. Every year, these are placed on the windowsill. I take the first shower. The smell of the campfire mixes with the steam and the verbena body wash and the lavender shampoo. Tiles in aqua and green, shaped like seashells. And above me, the citron-stained glass of an eagle.

Then the most important ritual. I grab my late mother's binoculars, and l go outside to the insanely big wooden deck to look at the Salish Sea. The Salish never disappoints. If I concentrate, the water moves in every direction. Always the same and always different. The water is bluish gray with eggshell edges. I stand with my elbows on the deck railing watching. Brine and creosote and rot. The breeze is soft as if someone is breathing on me. Ducks floating and diving and floating. For the hour my husband takes to shower and shave and organize the fridge, the water belongs solely to me. I can hear the prop planes from the tiny airport down the road. I'm wearing the same lemon colored dress I wear every year and that I only wear here. Here and nowhere else. It has a deep plunge in the back that lets in more sun. A faint smell of geranium from a neglected pot. Scrub jays are demanding dinner, and I fling peanuts on the roof. Sunflowers in an aqua bucket. The wood of the deck warms my bare feet. After a long winter of long pants and long sleeves and long raincoats, I have forgotten I have skin.

Later, we will have cocktails and dinner on the deck, balancing on the two rickety wicker chairs. And later still, we will be here looking at the water. Why look away or go inside? The water is so calm it appears to be glass, as if you could walk all the way to Sucia Island on it. The receding gray of the other islands: Patos and Matia. The chug of a red freighter inching along in the strait. A sunset to break your heart, coral and pink blooming from cerulean.

I grew up in an unpredictable house filled with anger, and I live in an increasingly unpredictable world filled with anger. Once a year, I need the permanence of the Salish. This is the cup I need to drink from all year long.

Smell the sea again. Smell the wood. The middle of July. Stop time.

My Tiny Pond

In my yard on Orcas Island, I have a pond. A broken fountain ensures that it stays murky and full of mosquitoes. Circled by droopy ferns and holly berry and dying grass. And a decrepit chain link fence meant to curb the bird carnage wrought by our two cats. In August, it is fascinating.

Because something changes every day. Something new yet expected. I have watched this pond three years in a row. I know what's coming next, but it's still extraordinary. In the world I inhabit, logic and science have become enemies of the people. So I find it reassuring to watch science at work in my pond.

I have to look closely, but even through the muck, I can see them. Eggs bundled like tapioca. The miracle of cell division in any egg. Simple and complex. Unseen by me. They wiggle out of their protective jelly. Then tail fins. Gills. I sit and I watch. Bloated black tadpoles. Swimming! Barely visible under the umber water.

Tadpoles are a wonder. Is there anything more magical? They gather closely, as a soccer team readying for a scrum. Tails forming. Tails receding. Tiny back legs appear, small as a bud on a tree. They tuck their legs under, delicately, demure ladies closing their fans. What must it feel like? To suddenly sprout legs? And not just sprout them but know, when the first two appear, to tuck them under so you can still swim? I watch and I watch and I watch. Herons will eat some. Snakes will eat some. Some will eat each other.

The survivors seem to transform overnight. Frogs appear, awkward in their new bodies, like a tween at a dance. Then, one day, I go to my pond and they are gone. Overnight, they have disappeared into the trees. I can hear them rasping, but I don't see them again.

August miracles from a clouded backyard pond.

Harley's Farm
by Michelle DiSarno

A wearying, sinuous road, but approaching Binghamton
always felt like morning. Riding alongside the farm's
neatly patterned plains was like a long, satisfied sigh.
Then Harley, four brooms in hand, would point us
to the tattered, peeling barn. As we swept out the milking parlor,
I sensed the transformation: oak floors, stuffed pantries,
a dining hall and bunks for the masses.

We were tempted to pretend we were children
growing up there, building forts out of hay bales,
letting the swim hole zip up our bodies. We felt
we deserved these simple earthly things. But Harley watched,

outside with us if he could, coughing, his liver boiling
with old heroin residue, his imagination full
of the kids he was going to share his stories with,
the troubled ones who would come to breathe
the corn-stalk, dew-grass, free air.

And so there was Mark welding metal, me swinging
the ax, cringing at my calluses, Ken with his hand
on the plow, rubbing some precise disc in his back,
and Jess sealing in the fiberglass—promised warmth.

Rest replenishes but does not rewind. Around the firepit
Harley patted our backs, said he couldn't wait to see it
all done, but we knew. Ashes lifted and disintegrated.
How is it that the soul just understands

when something is over?—like a solemn nod,
the release of a muscle, a steady drone in the stomach.
Amid the crackling, Harley silently passed the burden
to us, and we accepted, as naturally as breathing.
And the barn, a shadow blending into night, reminded me
of how we must work for ends we can't see yet.

The Call of the North
by Brenda Wilbee

I boarded Skagway's fast ferry to see about a new job in Haines, driving tourists into grizzly country. I'd been coming to Alaska for several years as a tour bus driver. The Call of the North had tapped my shoulder. Larger than life, this vast territory and tundra, untamed.

Normally, I drive tourists up White Pass out of Skagway, Alaska, a small town caught in a crevice between two ridiculously high mountain ranges, and then wind them down into the Canadian tundra, landscapes unrolling into boreal forests and glacial lakes. But the summer of 2014, I'd taken a job with the new company in town—unfortunately, it came with expectations that didn't suit. A job posted on our grocery store bulletin, however, caught my eye. WILD ADVENTURES IN HAINES, it read. Taking tourists out to a grizzly reserve. Why not?

The fast ferry's engine hummed underfoot, and with fifty or sixty fellow passengers, I chugged south on the world's deepest fjord to Skagway's neighbor forty-five minutes away. Surrounding mountains rose up 6,000 feet. Walruses lunged up onto barnacle-clad rocks, slapped the stone, and settled into naps and snores. A whale nearby surfaced and breached. I jumped backward and laughed with strangers over getting splattered. Then the long walk off the pier to town, onto Main Street, turn left on Third.

"Hey, I'm here!" I announced, finding Wild Adventure's office and letting myself in.

"Hey, hi!" A blonde, twenty-something woman looked up from a cluttered desk. "You must be Brenda. I'm Traci. Welcome."

A bit of chitchat, then down to business.

"I'll have you go out with Kits today. She's a seasoned driver, and she knows all the tricks. But her tour isn't for an hour. Let me show you around."

The usual dog-eared employee housing. Ah, a dining room. Meal tickets available. So far, so good.

"I'll take you out to the barn," said Traci, her yellow ponytail bobbing as she tripped through a graveled yard of buttercups and weeds and stepped into a large, rusty, corrugated tin shed. Five buses inside. Not the sleek motor coaches of Holland America-Princess I was used to. Nor the cute little twenty-four-seaters of smaller companies I'd gotten used to. These were retired school buses someone had bought off a sales rack in the Lower 48. Driving them would be an adventure of its own.

We found Kits doing a precheck on a bus she called Sorenson. "I'm sore when I'm in it," she explained.

"Haha."

She was a middle-aged, retired park ranger who'd worked in national parks all over the United States. Yosemite, Yellowstone, Grand Canyon. "But nothing comes close to Alaska," she said, thick braid falling off her shoulder. "So I keep coming up here. Summers are my fix."

"Same here." My own addiction in the open. Over-the-top scenery, ridiculously fresh air, friends so unlike me—I can never get enough of quirky.

Traci left Kits to take over.

"It helps to be alpha for this tour," Kits warned. "People's lives depend on their respect for you. Not to worry, just watch and learn. Wanna help me check that left taillight?"

We rattled down to the pier, every joint of Sorenson squealing in arthritic pain. We got out. Held up our tour signs so people could find us. About twenty gathered.

Arms crossed, Kits stood at the bus door, and without a whole lot of "Where are you from?" she jumped in. "Brenda and I are taking you up to Chilkoot Lake, where grizzlies roam. Can't guarantee you'll see one, they don't keep a schedule. But nine days out of ten, they're around. Do what I say, and we might have a shot of surviving a close encounter."

They all laughed nervously. Me too. Boom, just like that, she'd put herself in charge.

"Seriously," she said. "Do what I say, when I say, and we're golden. Got that?"

They nodded.

"Jump."

No one jumped.

"Geez, you're all dead meat. Let's try this again. Simon says tap your head and stomp your feet."

This time, they tapped their heads and stomped.

"Alight-alright-*alrighty then!*" she rolled out like Matthew McConaughey. And while singing "The Bear Went Over the Mountain," we boarded.

She snaked north, away from Lynn Canal and into the Tongass National Rainforest, tossing off her shoulder the usual tourist stuff—"On the right . . . On the left . . ."—interjecting the do's and don'ts of running into bears.

"If it's brown, lay down. If it's black, fight back. If it's white, goodnight." She had them repeat the formula.

"The reserve," she went on, "is their foraging route. These grizzlies, technically called brown bears, circle daily, sometimes twice. We know who they are, but we steer clear. Observe from afar. This is their turf we're visiting, and, so far, knock on wood"—she knocked her head—"no fatalities."

Weak laughter.

"A few emergency airlifts, though, to Seattle and Anchorage." Delivered as "small print," guffaws ignited to blow out the windows.

We came to a stop at Chilkoot Lake. Pristine stillness. Not a ripple. I thought of Lake Louise in Banff National Park. This lake was not turquoise—but it was nonetheless stunning.

We followed Kits past a walkway leading down to the lake and veered left instead into the usual suspects of a temperate rainforest: Sitka spruce, western hemlock, yellow cedar, red cedar, mountain hemlock, shore pine. The cedar trees towered so high and so tightly together that sunlight could only dapple through. A quiet place except for the squirrels and birds, branches snapping. I thought of childhood fairytale woods. This was them. Anything could happen.

Kits halted when we came to a hushed glen. We fell in, facing her. The dappled sunlight spilling through the green danced atop a pine-needle carpet, and somewhere overhead, a woodpecker rat-a-tat-tatted twenty-five blows a second.

"Tongass National Rainforest," Kits said, "is the largest temperate rainforest in the world, comprising seventeen million acres, eighty-nine percent of which—"

A ginormous brown grizzly padded out of the woods and paused five yards behind Kits. I froze. Two cubs tumbled out of the brush behind her. I stopped breathing, but Kits kept talking, and the giant sow pulled up on her hind feet, sniffing the air, ears alert. I could not move; I could not speak.

"B . . . b . . . bbb . . ." someone behind me stuttered.

"B-bb . . ." someone else tried.

I tried, too, but the enormity of the bear—six yards from where I stood—shut down all brain signals. She was too big, too close, too tall. Nine feet? Her nose quivered. I could see the grizzled fur of her chin. She held her front paws at chest level, claws hidden. Oh my god. I wavered on my feet.

"B . . . b . . . *bear*!" someone finally spit out.

Kits turned ever so slowly. Ever so slowly, she turned back with an ashen face.

"I want you to walk slowly toward the bus. No running, no talking. If you do what I say, this is not a problem," she said with tranquility to contradict fright. "There you go, I'm right behind you. That's it, no running, stay quiet, you're doing great . . ."

I focused on her voice, a melodic calm to my chaotic shock and just enough to get my legs moving. But what if someone panicked? Or had a heart attack? What if someone broke into a run, all of us panicking? She kept talking, and I matched my steps to an imaginary clock ticking in my head. *Tick tick*, waiting for the *tock* to snuff the life right out of me. Where was the bear? Still on her feet? Had she dropped to all fours? Was she tracking us? I wanted to turn to check if I was safe, but I kept walking, keeping my eyes on the path in front of me so my feet wouldn't tangle and down I'd go. The bus hove into view. Run! No! One foot, another foot. *Tick tick tick tick.*

Finally, we got to the old yellow school bus, and I collapsed into my seat. No *tock*. I was fine. I was alive.

Kits had done a remarkable job. All in a day's work, she told us, humoring us out of our scare and psyching all but one of us into going back outside. This time, she led us along the river. Carefully, we walked the trail while she showed us distant berry patches and river crossings these grizzlies traveled.

I didn't take the job. Not enough alpha in me. One panicked tourist was all it would take for a grizzly to dine fine. I'd rather scoop ice cream at Skagway's Kone Company.

A few days later, I found a job with Southeast Tours and went back to threading tourists through Skagway's White Pass, up and over the Cascade Mountains, and down into the Canadian Yukon, where black bears roam.

"Hey, boys and girls," I said first day on the job. "When is a black bear not a black bear?"

No guesses hazarded.

"When they're brown, cinnamon, sometimes blue. We even have a white one, I hear."

I wound us off the summit, down into the tortuous valley of moonscape rubble and surrounding mountains, their pockets riddled with glaciers. Just past Log Cabin of old Gold Rush days, I drove into the marshland.

"We actually have *three* kinds of bears up here," I went on. "Black bears, brown bears, and—whoa, whoa, whoa!" I choked, pumping hard on the brakes. Big Red, my bus, threatened to swerve out from under me. A moose had just lumbered out of the boreal forest and marsh to stand in the middle of the highway.

Enormous and balanced atop spindly legs, antlers five feet across, there she was, all but eyeball-to-eyeball when I finally came to a stop. Crazy, unpredictable, lightning fast, moose can be dangerous. We'd take a heavy hit if she decided to charge. My guests went wild. They took pictures. I idled, hazards on. If not alpha, I was at least beta.

"What's the third kind of bear?" asked the man sitting behind me.

"Gummy bears! They. of course, come in all colors, red, yellow, green . . ."

Guffaws to burst out the windows.

Scars on Souls
by Nadia Boulos

school bell rings
this is not a drill
uniforms gather in the yard
aimlessly running around
scrambling to find a familiar face

i stand in the middle
aghast
i hear screams and cries
but I can't move
as if crushed by an incubus

finally I'm found
relieved, I get in the car

the freeway is empty
i've never seen it so empty
flipped cars on fire
to my left then to my right

the quiet around me a sharp blade
cutting through violable breath

we make it home

pictures of burning cars
linger in my mind
burning grooves into gray matter
branding me a child of war

i still dread the silence
and empty freeways

Surely the Presence
by Amory Peck

Today, EvergreenHealth Medical Center is a major complex of
hospital services in Kirkland, Washington. Opened as a small
seventy-six-bed facility in 1972, Evergreen sits on a hill
overlooking I-405, easily seen from the freeway. However, until I
became a patient, I didn't take any particular notice as I drove past
it regularly. Then, in September 1978, I checked in as a patient.
The hospital had been created to be a beacon of hope, health, and
repair. As I entered the medical facility that fall day, I was too
scared to have any of those positive feelings. I was thirty-five
years old, had cancer, and was about to have my right breast
removed.

Some say thirty-five is the beginning of middle age. Most say
forty. I just know that I wasn't feeling like any sort of adult. I was
frightened and grateful my mother and twenty-three-year-old
brother had flown in from Michigan to be with me.

1978 was a pivotal time to face a mastectomy. Until shortly
before, speaking of breast cancer was taboo. Remnants of old-
fashioned modesty and reluctance to speak of a woman's bosom in
polite society put such cancer into the shadows. That misplaced
sensitivity had begun to disappear. In 1974, Betty Ford, former

First Lady, spoke openly about her breast cancer and the resulting radical mastectomy. Her words brought the disease into the open. A phenomenon known as the Betty Ford Blip occurred, with record numbers of women seeking mammograms following her address to the nation.

I had been looking for medical help for several years, ever since I discovered quite a large lump in my right breast. The doctor to whom I was assigned didn't take it seriously. At one point, he said to me, "I'd have to cut off the whole breast to get rid of a lump of that size." Years later, I talked with a lawyer about suing that incompetent and insensitive physician. He explained that I really didn't have a case since I had survived.

In the early fall of 1978, having changed medical insurance plans and been assigned to a new, helpful, and ready-to-take-action doctor, my cancer was diagnosed. I found his name, Dr. Magoo, amusing, for I couldn't erase images of the extremely myopic Mr. Magoo of cartoon fame from my mind. Despite the silliness about his name, my physician became my lifesaver.

In the four years between Betty Ford's surgery and mine, a different approach was used to remove the cancer. Mrs. Ford had a radical mastectomy, which, along with removing the breast, took the muscles of the chest wall and all the lymph nodes under the arm. I, instead, had a modified radical mastectomy, which removed the breast but saved the muscles of the chest wall and took only a sampling of the nodes. More changes in treatment were coming. I remember Dr. Magoo saying, "There's a new procedure called a lumpectomy, but it is just now being tried. We have no data on success rates, and I'm too concerned about that to recommend it to you."

Entering Evergreen, I wasn't surprised to be assigned to a shared room. It was, as expected, small with a thin curtain separating the two beds. My roommate had arrived earlier, so she had the window side of the room. I did not, however, expect my roommate's three visitors to be smoking. Unbelievably, the patient was smoking, too. The stench in the room, especially with my already queasy stomach, was awful. By today's standards, that's unimaginable. Then, it was acceptable.

My mother turned Mama Bear. Muttering, "This will not do," she left the room abruptly. I was quickly reassigned to a private room. Mother promised, "If insurance won't cover the cost of a private room, your father and I will." (Note: There was no extra charge for them to pay.)

Today, a patient generally checks in the morning of surgery. In 1978, I had to check in the afternoon before. All my pre-surgery work was completed by 4 p.m. There was no chance of going home, though. I'd been admitted and was there to stay. The hours ahead seemed endless, with nothing to do except worry. But then my friends started arriving. It was wonderfully distracting to have them with me. My boss and good friend, Barbara, was there. My friend Linda, who had been with me during the biopsy and also when I learned the result was malignant, was in the room. My across-the-hall neighbor, Sue, arrived, as well as work-friend Sue. Mother and brother, of course. There were, perhaps, ten people with me.

"There are too many of you in this room," a passing nurse declared. My heart sank; I was certain my friends would be asked to leave. Then the nurse said, "Follow me."

The room she led us to seemed multipurpose. It was definitely used for storage, and there were a number of folding chairs around, making me think staff meetings probably took place there, too. Several wheelchairs were parked against the wall. It was the sort of catch-all space found in most office buildings, the holding place where old equipment goes to die. Whatever its usual use, it was ours for the time being. The extra space was a gift, and the permission to be together a blessing.

My mother, skilled at leading meetings, organized us into a circle, and my filled-with-nervous-energy brother slung the chairs into place. After that task, Ed was drawn to the wheelchairs. He spent a goodly amount of time perfecting his ability to do wheelies in a wheelchair. Friends kept arriving until I had about twenty supporters in the room. Despite my fear and the concern of everyone around me, there was laughter and good-natured bantering. There were also more than a few tears shed. My pastor, Reverend William Welch, part of the gaggle of people in the room, called us to prayer. We held hands around the circle, and he prayed: for me, the surgeons and nurses, for health and healing, for calm. Those linked hands and the words of the prayer brought calm to me. That makeshift room, with its jumble of stored equipment and mismatched folding chairs, became holy space.

Several days later, as I was finishing up my stay at Evergreen, one of my nurses said to me, "I passed by the meeting room where you and your friends were gathered and stood there a moment as you prayed. The spirit of the Lord was surely with you."

Forty-six years later, I can still conjure up the safety, security, and peace I felt in that cluttered space, in the midst of the bustling, sterile hospital. I'd had encounters with the holy before, at church camp around the campfire, for example. But, that evening, in the middle of hospital detritus, I felt, more than ever before, the certainty of the promise, "Whenever two or three are gathered in my name, I am with them." The circle of clasped hands, the love, the determination to buoy me up, Pastor Bill's strong, compelling voice—surely the presence of the Lord was in that room.

How Many Ways Can I Praise the Hundred Acre Wood
by Taya Kesslau

I listen with the perked ears of a black-tailed doe
cupped to the sonic world like a seashell
holding echoes of the ocean.
The ocean of life in the wooded realm.

I cast my delight outward over waves
of birdsong, fernsong, tree dirt cone web
brushsong. Breaking open in wonder
weeping for joy song.

I cast my delight outward for red bark
for green lacy boughs, for bursting yellow
buttercups, for bugs that go like little clocks.

My delight is a red plump berry glistening
on a forest vine swallowed in green and green
and verdant filtered sunlight.

My delight is a keen-eyed creature swooping
to pluck and gobble a ripe red berry.

My bones ring with kinship with the tall thin trees
the tall thick trees with the overstory canopies.

Amber sap flows through my veins
through vessel cells through xylem cells

delivering jubilance ferrying nourishment
nutrients up out throughout all of us living creatures
standing crawling ticking flying floating lying leaping
in praise in these Hundred Acre Wood.

Ghost Stories
by Evelyn Fletcher Symes

The rain leaves the pastures sparkling with droplets captured in the grassy hummocks. He looks at his wife. They smile knowingly at the thunder of their daughter's steps as she careens down the stairs into the kitchen.

"Sun's out," she announces breathlessly.

"'Tis," he says winking at her mother.

This elicits a huff of exasperation from the girl. "Come on. Let's go." Her voice is whiny with impatience.

The ice in his glass of tea tinkles as he sets it down. "Where?" he says.

She rolls her eyes. "Dad," she intones, "come on."

"Be dark in an hour or so," he says, looking out the window. "Not much time left, Annie."

"You know we find more after it rains," she counters petulantly.

"All right. All right," he says and stands, stretching his arms above his head.

Their small ranch on the Red was once the site of an oil boomtown. In 1918, more than twenty thousand souls drilled down through the surrounding prairie, looking for elusive pools of oil. Many lost their lives. Most lost their money and their hope. All that remains of their greed-driven plundering is the occasional rose bush or iris bed lost among the returning prairie grasses and the faint tracks of their roads. The ghosts of their brief sojourn lie hidden along these fading lanes. Soon, even these will be gone as nature reclaims what they despoiled.

A sharp wind wafts in the window, ruffling the curtains, just as it ruffled the curtains of the forgotten thousands who once lived in tarpaper shacks and remain as ghosts.

Annie takes his hand and pulls him toward the door. He lets her tug him along with little resistance. She chatters, recalling their previous plunder, housed in jars and shoeboxes beneath her bed, guarded by the discarded plush animals and dolls she heaps on her pillows each morning, as yet unwilling to relegate them to a box in the attic with her yellowed baby clothes.

"Maybe we'll find another gold piece. Or a Mercury dime."

"Or a china doll's head," he says. "Remember Myrtle? We found her after the Easter storm."

She wrinkles her nose at this. "It was cracked, thrown away. No one lost it."

"*How* it got cracked was the mystery," he says, reminding her of the story they'd fashioned for Myrtle's poor broken head: discarded when diphtheria took the little girl who loved her.

"Broken dolls are not valuable," she says, flaunting her new worldliness. "They're too sad," she adds in a whisper.

They walk through the sodden grass, his pants rain-damp and cool against his legs. He wonders how long Myrtle will be allowed to lodge in the shoebox under her bed with no story, no connection to the little girl who loved her so long ago.

When they arrive at the track, he stops and looks up at the pink-faced clouds, remnants of the first fall storm scudding across the sky, as though fearful of being left behind by their swollen cumulus parents. Annie, head down, sees only the fresh-washed sand at her feet. He sighs and releases her. She begins a careful surveillance of the path. They walk along together. The earlier winds have stopped, and the few remaining birds who haven't left on their migration call back and forth, tentatively seeking the reassurance of each other's presence.

"Look," he says and squats to better see what the rain's revealed.

"What is it?" She squats next to him.

Her legs lost their chubby roundness last winter and are newly slender, strangely out of sync with the freshly revealed, bony knobs of her knees. He smiles. Her mother worried she would take after her side of the family, short, plump, and relegated to the eternally youthful, descriptive *cute*. That fear's purged. A new one, peopled with boys, cars, and whispered secrets, awaits them.

"Look," he says. He digs his finger into the soil under a faint circle and pries loose a ring.

"Daddy!" she gasps.

He rubs it, smoothing the dirt from its surface, revealing the dull gleam of gold, and drops it on her palm. Biting her lip as she always does when concentrating, Annie polishes it. A second, smaller ring lies where it was hidden beneath the larger one.

"This must've been hers," he says, slipping it on his little finger, wagging it at her.

"She was small," his daughter notes, falling unwittingly into the search for the story.

She slides the ring from his finger onto hers. It halts on the middle joint. Not to be deterred, she pops the recalcitrant digit in her mouth and slides the ring through the resultant slick, over the offending cartilage, to settle at the base of her finger. Then she slides the larger ring over the smaller one and clenches her fist to keep both safe.

They walk, their steps slow, their heads down, searching.

"How could they *both* be lost?" she begins, "Together?"

"Good question," he responds.

"Maybe she accidentally tossed them out," she continues, "put them in a dish while she was fixing dinner, and they got knocked into the slop bucket."

"Both?" he asks.

"Right." She draws the word out, assessing the probability. "Right," she affirms. "It's the two together that's the mystery."

He nods his agreement. "Life has many mysteries."

"And in a road," she ruminates. "How in a road?" They walk a while longer.

She sucks in her breath, shocked at a new notion. "The death wagon? Could they have both died and been picked up by the death wagon, the rings falling . . ." She stops and shakes her head. "The rings wouldn't have been left on the bodies."

"No," he agrees. "Family, grave diggers, body collectors, they check for valuables. I suppose *they* could be the ones who lost them—after scavenging them."

She snorts her disregard for this suggestion. "Scavengers would have a tight grip on anything gold, Dad."

He taps her clenched fist. "Proof's in the pudding," he says. They laugh.

Annie loosens her grip and takes his hand. Savoring the promise of the story hovering over the rain-soaked land, they walk on. Farther down the track, he spies the wine-stained smudge of a late-summer iris peeking through the wild prairie grasses. The blooms are all that remain of one woman's story here—that and the collapsed steps that lead nowhere.

"So," he says, prompting her. "Lost, or deliberate?"

This stops her. She looks down at their hands, quickly releasing his to look more closely at the rings. "Deliberate?" she intones in astonishment. "But it's gold." He looks at her and raises his eyebrows. "But . . ." she says and stops. "Proof's in the pudding?" she says uncertainly.

He shrugs and walks on, his hands resting in his pockets.

"But it's gold, Dad."

"Do people *lose* gold?" he asks.

They walk a while longer. Bran, her father's hunting dog, runs up to them from ranging across the pasture, pushes his nose roughly against her clenched fist, snorts, and charges back across the field, bounding over hummocks, searching for rabbits, ignoring the ghosts they seek.

She looks at her hand and then at the bounding dog. "Sooo," she says, drawing out the word. "If they weren't lost, it's a different question."

"Have to be," he says, letting her find her way into the story.

They continue walking. The track narrows. He moves ahead, looking back from time to time, checking to see she's not falling too far behind. She lags. He stops and watches her as she meanders through the verge and back to the middle of the track, unaware of his protective presence.

"Why?" She looks up at him.

He smiles. "Good question."

He watches her as she closes the gap between them, wondering where her story will take her.

"Something must have been more valuable," she says as she reaches him.

"Must have been," he agrees.

"To throw away two gold rings," she muses. "Wedding rings." She stops and turns to him, "Wedding rings that have been worn." She holds up her hand and removes the rings. "See, there are marks."

"I noticed that," he says. "They were worn a good while."

"Before," she says.

"Before they weren't," he says.

She looks at the rings lying in her palm, her brows drawn together in reluctant understanding. "Here, Daddy," she says, slipping the rings into his pocket. "They didn't belong together anymore, did they? They weren't connected. They had to let each other go."

He puts his arm around her and pulls her to him. She nestles her face into his side. "Their story is so sad," she mumbles into his shirt.

"I know, Annie," he says, thinking of the blooms she will leave behind.

A Hundred Acre Wood
by Linda Conroy

This forest is in town, close
to those who live in one small room,
so near to noise, to banter, competition.

Close to those who rarely touch a leaf,
or watch a rabbit freeze beneath a scarlet bloom,
or in the market's busy blur of action
see a deer tuck its young behind a bush of evergreen.

All creatures scatter in the turn of light
and though these paths are modest, unrefined
we can take care not to disrupt
the flow of nature's plan

take care while being self-absorbed,
to give thanks for the magic sun
shining through a geometry of leaves.

No Place Like Home
by Marth Oliver-Smith

Driving to my waitress job on Interstate 5 between Ashland and Medford, Oregon, one August afternoon in 1972, I smelled hot metal and heard the engine of my VW bus ticking like a manic alarm clock. Before the car died in the middle of the right lane, I managed to guide it off the road and onto a patchy, narrow shoulder. Once out of the bus, I stood immobilized in the dust and desiccated weeds populating the ground where the shoulder merged with the scabrous, dried-out landscape of the Rogue Valley.

August in the Rogue Valley can be brutally hot, and that day it must have been 105, though the number on the thermometer made no difference after a certain point. Star thistle, foxtails, and parched, mangy grasses were the only signs of anything living, though I thought about rattlesnakes.

The nearest phone was about two miles back in Talent or more than a mile ahead in Phoenix. It was at least another seven miles to work in Medford and maybe six back home to Ashland—too far to walk to either place, especially in the heat. I couldn't move, couldn't think.

In a stasis of indecision, my thoughts kept spooling back to the reasons I was in this place, this moment, this situation. I knew why I was standing marooned in hell on the side of the freeway, heading to a shitty waitress job at Stanley's Family Restaurant. It was because eight years ago I had hopped into bed with Will, my boyfriend, now husband, when I was eighteen, a freshman in college with no particular plan or purpose in life except to be free of my mother and her third husband. Desperate to get out from under their iron reign, I hadn't consciously intended to escape through pregnancy and emergency marriage, but that's what it came down to. I wasn't thinking about consequences at the time.

I believed my purgatorial waitress job had to be one of hell's waiting rooms, but I was actually glad to get away from a scene that had been unfolding in a cramped little house on Oak Street in Ashland, where Will and I and our three small children had been living for the last six weeks with another couple, friends we'd known from college, Cassie and Dan, and their two children. "Stay with us until you get settled," they had said.

What was supposed to have been a happy reunion with dear old friends turned into a dreary soap opera. Before we even arrived, it seemed Will and Cassie had rekindled an old affair they had started years before, which Dan and I knew nothing about. Dan and I were now doing an awkward dance around Cassie and Will, who had not quite decided how things were going to play out for all of us.

Not only was life strained with tension and drama, but we were broke. After our cross-country journey, we had about $200 left from Will's last paycheck.

Will decided not to apply for teaching jobs; he wanted to play guitar and keyboard in a country rock band some musician friends of Cassie and Dan had put together. They had started rehearsing and looking for gigs, but there was no income, of course. That's when I understood that I needed a job. I found one at Stanley's Family Restaurant in Medford, which was why I was sweltering on this desolate freeway shoulder with my feet burning up in my skimpy sandals. How I hated this place—the mountains, the dry, exhausting heat, the dust, the stunted vegetation, the giant, relentless western blue sky. This place was not my home. It was my nemesis, my enemy.

As I stood there beside the wounded van on I-5, I wondered if I had reached the end of something. The road? A chapter? Life as I knew it? But railing at my present situation was futile as cars sped by me. I was going to be late to work if I didn't figure out something immediately. I reflected grimly that I wasn't even much of a waitress since my only experience had been in a small coffee house in Boston called The Turk's Head, where I wore a miniskirt and boots and served espressos and Italian sodas to the sounds of folk musicians strumming and singing on a tiny stage. In the two weeks I had worked at Stanley's, I learned to please customers who liked their prime rib well done, medium, medium rare, almost raw, or burnt; I encountered customers who walked out without paying or sent food back to the kitchen two or three times. I served busloads of elderly tourists returning from gambling trips to Reno who arrived five minutes before closing time to order full dinners, all wanting separate checks and never leaving tips. I served tables of six who ordered pots of hot water for the teabags they had brought for the occasion—no tips.

Now standing in the unbearable sun, I thought of The Acorns, my grandmother's house in Rhode Island, where I had spent much of my childhood. My mother, on one of her sojourns with a new husband, would park my siblings and me there, sometimes for years and always in the summers. The old house had once been a grand place, though it was run-down and ramshackle. I still missed its comfortable shabbiness, its wide green lawn, the oak and dogwood trees, the brambly woods around the house. I thought of the ocean just a few miles from the house, where I spent most of my days lounging at the beach and riding waves. I thought of rainy days and the damp, dense green Rhode Island summers. Nothing green here in the Rogue Valley, no shade, no ocean for hundreds of miles, and suffocating mountain barriers all around.

A rusty black van skidded to a stop a few yards beyond my steaming bus, puncturing my reverie and spraying a layer of fine dust over me. The driver leaned across the passenger seat and rolled down his window.

"You wanna ride? Hop in, I'll take you where you wanna go. We ain't in a hurry."

I had never hitchhiked before, but I thought I might die out there. Against everything I'd ever been taught about getting into a car with a stranger, I climbed into the van. It wasn't a decision; I just did it, hopped right in. Doing something without thinking it through was a habit of mine.

Settled uneasily in the passenger bucket seat of the grungy van, I eyed the unevenly tinted side and back windows that looked like whoever had done the job had been doing acid. Streaks and dribbles made the glass look warped as if we were underwater. The driver—an aging hippie, possibly forty, which seemed old to me at twenty-six—was sporting the usual uniform: ratty ponytail, red bandanna, necklace of beads and feathers, bleary tattoos on both arms, with an extra flourish stuck through his earlobe—a porcupine quill?

The van's back seats had been removed and replaced with a sheet of plywood and a foam pad covered in a grimy, faded, but still lurid fabric of poisonous-looking orange and purple flowers. Untethered and unbuckled, a little boy and a small goat surfed freely in the space behind me.

"Name's Shasta, after the mountain, ya know," said my friendly rescuer-possibly-kidnapper. "Used to be Bill. And the boy is Nebula—Neb we call him. Goat's Capricorn."

As we pulled onto the freeway, I felt a jab of anxiety that Shasta Bill might not take me to Stanley's Family Restaurant. He might keep driving past Medford into the parched wilds of Central Point or Gold Hill. I knew there were all kinds of people living out there—survivalists and gun hoarders, drug dealers, wild therapy groups, religious cults and communes—maybe this guy was a Charlie Manson fan. Who knew? The Manson trial had only ended a year ago. I imagined people finding the abandoned VW bus on the side of I-5 hours from when I'd been kidnapped. I decided not to be afraid. Yes, I was taking a risk, but Shasta Bill seemed less alien to me at the moment than my own husband. Will, who was risking much more with our whole family than I was climbing into a stranger's beat-up hippie van.

I glanced behind me at Little Neb. Wearing only a pair of grungy underpants, he was bouncing around with the goat in the back of the van. Chewing on an old popsicle stick, he leaned forward and breathed over my shoulder. Sticky orange popsicle drizzle mixed with dust had dried on the bare skin of his round little belly. The goat smelled like goats smell, strong and musky, but it was all mixed in with man-sweat, cloying orange popsicle, and profound grunge. They stared at me, the boy with large, curious brown eyes, and the goat with eyes of pale, indifferent blue, the only sign of cold in the immediate universe.

Shasta Bill was one of the Mt. Shasta vortex hippies. Many spiritual seekers had settled in the Siskiyou Mountains, in Ashland

and other parts of the Rogue Valley, in the late '60s. Shasta was one of the places with "vibes." The vortex in Gold Hill, a town a few miles north of Medford, where Shasta Bill was heading, was the site of The Oregon House of Mystery, an old tourist attraction from the 1920s that consisted of a funky shack with a mysterious gravitational force field half above and half below the ground. Somewhere between the vortices of Mt. Shasta and Gold Hill, the seekers expected to discover their bliss. I wasn't looking for bliss, and even if I were, I had no idea where to find it. I just wanted a place to live, a home, a place to be myself, whoever that was.

I relaxed a little when Shasta Bill pulled off the freeway at the Medford exit onto Riverside Avenue, a long one-way strip of funky bars, burger and pizza joints, industrial parking lots, tire stores, gas stations, repair shops, and second-hand stores shimmering in the heat and grit of the dry and, to me, still alien Western air.

As we approached Stanley's ugly, brown, 1950s space-age building, I felt a sick, panicky feeling. For a moment, I wanted to tell Shasta Bill to keep driving—take me with him. I could just go live at the commune or wherever he lived. I could go with him and little Neb and the goat. Couldn't I? But I would never do that. Though I sometimes fantasized about escaping from my life with Will, I was not like my mother. I would never leave my children as she had each time she got divorced and remarried.

In Stanley's parking, lot I thanked Shasta Bill for the ride; he flashed a mossy-toothed grin and a peace sign. Little Nebula waved his sticky palm, and the goat butted its head against the side window as the van pulled away. I would never see them again, but I wouldn't forget them.

At the restaurant, I made a quick call to Will from the pay phone in the room where the waitresses changed and smoked during the five-minute breaks we were allowed on a slow night. Then I changed identities from imitation hippie mom in cut-off jeans, black tee shirt, and sandals to imitation waitress, hair pulled back in a ponytail, wearing a mustard yellow uniform, tiny apron, and grease-spotted sneakers. But who was I really? I didn't know.

Until two weeks ago, I had prided myself on being "normal" and "not my mother." I would be better than she was at being a wife and a mother. Now here I was, failing at my marriage to Will, and, like her, a distracted mother. But for this moment in time, my life was the Stanley's specials and getting my orders into the moody, ill-humored cooks who could sabotage you by delaying your order, overcooking the prime rib, or suddenly running out of the dessert special.

As I moved among the customers, taking orders and delivering dishes, I had a terrible sense that in fact this *was* my real and only life. The life I had lived for twenty-six years was a pale and fading star, drifting out beyond this universe. My life as the girl from Rhode Island who spent most of her childhood in a big, old house called The Acorns and went to many schools, a life of not really paying attention to signs or following directions, not listening to the warning voices, the life with Will and the children—that life, those lives—were but half-remembered dreams in the hours of waiting tables at Stanley's.

When I had stood immobilized and powerless, in a stupor on the side of the freeway in the relentless glaring sun that August day, I had perhaps reached the end of something. Over the next few weeks and months, I began to recognize that while there were endings to roads and chapters, there could be beginnings, too, new paths to choose and take on my own.

The first sign of this change in perspective was that my vision of the Rogue Valley as a desiccated, green-starved landscape shifted. I learned where to look for oases of vegetation and waterways. I took my children to Ashland's Lithia Park where Ashland Creek winds its way to the Rogue River and eventually joins the Pacific Ocean, whose glory I would come to appreciate in a different way from my own Atlantic coast. I grew to love the Siskiyou Mountains as they turned shades of purple in a sunset. I found new colors everywhere—subtle shades of green in the trees and vegetation, deep red in the bark of the Manzanita and the peeling red-brown skin and lime-green underbark of the Madrones. My resistance to this place that seemed like purgatory gradually dissolved. I discovered that I had the power to be at home there, if not to find my "bliss," then to take control of my life and live it on my own terms.

Contributors & Editors

M'Lyn Avera (contributor) is a writer, visual artist and teacher who lives on the traditional lands of the Lummi and Nooksack tribes, known as Bellingham, Washington, with her rescue dog, Hope. Her work is included in *True Stories Anthology* volumes VI and VII. M'Lyn is currently working on a memoir.

Born in Lebanon, **Nadia Boulos** (contributor) moved to the United States in 2001 and now lives in Bellingham with her family. A Western Washington University graduate in Business Marketing, she founded Reset Web Design. Her experiences of Lebanon's civil war inspire her writing. Nadia enjoys yoga, hiking, music, travel, and family time.

Nancy Canyon (contributor), MFA, is a widely published artist and author. Her work can be seen in *The Madrona Project, I Sing the Salmon Home, Spring and All, Raven Chronicles, Whatcom Writes,* and more. She coaches for The Narrative Project and teaches through Chuckanut Writers. Her memoir, *Struck: A Season on a Fire Lookout,* as well as *Celia's Heaven* (fiction) and *Saltwater* (poetry), are available at Village Books.

Susan Chase-Foster (contributor & editor) travels the world but lives mostly in Bellingham, Washington, and Interior Alaska.

She's a passionate poem penner, word and watercolor journaler, and obsessive camera clicker. Her work has appeared in *Cirque, Alaska Women Speak, Heron Clan,* and numerous anthologies, and in *Xiexie Taipei,* her collection of poems from Taipei.

Linda Conroy (contributor), a retired social worker, writes about the complexities of human nature and our connection to the natural world. She enjoys facilitating writing groups at Village Books. Her poems have appeared in various journals and anthologies. She is the author of two poetry collections, *Ordinary Signs* and *Familiar Sky.*

Eileen Coughlin (contributor) has an EdD in Educational Psychology and an MFA in creative writing. Her poems have been published in *Awakenings Review, Door is a Jar, Literary Mama,* and *Better Than Starbucks.* Her book *Postcards from Autism* is being published by Kelsay Books and is due for release in 2025.

Sheila Dearden (contributor) is an author, naturalist, voiceover artist, and beekeeper. A lover of the outdoors, she lives in the Pacific Northwest. She holds a master's degree in environmental education and certification as a marine naturalist. Her memoir-in-progress, *Uprooted: A Natural History of Home,* explores connections between landscape, home, and the human heart.

Michelle DiSarno (contributor) is a teacher, photographer, and poet from New Jersey. Her work has been featured in *Fathom Magazine, Pine Row Press, Humana Obscura,* and *The Platform Review.* She strives to celebrate the beauty of life, even with all its aches and longings. She occasionally posts on Instagram: @inperfectwander.

Randall Dills (editor) is a poet based on Fidalgo Island near La Conner, Washington. He is the author of *The Universe at the Point* *of Contraction* (FutureCycle Press). He's published widely and is a supporter of PEN International, serving as a representative on its Young People's Committee.

Victoria Doerper (contributor & editor) writes creative nonfiction and poetry from her cottage near the Salish Sea in Bellingham, Washington. Find her work in her book *What if We All Bloomed: Poems of Nature, Love, and Aging*, as well as in literary publications like *Crocodile Quarterly, I Sing the Salmon Home*, and *Orion*.

Seán Thomas Dwyer (contributor & editor) is the author of a memoir, *A Quest for Tears: Surviving Traumatic Brain Injury*, and his short work has been anthologized in more than a dozen publications. He is the host of the Village Books Open Mic in Bellingham, Washington, as well as the podcast The 1320 Books.

Marian Exall (contributor & editor) is an award-winning author of mystery and historical fiction. Born and educated in England, she lived in France and Belgium before moving to the United States. In September 2024, Marian returned to England to attend the Historical Novel Society's conference at Dartington Hall in Devon.

Evelyn Fletcher Symes (contributor) carries on her family's long tradition of storytelling. Her stories have been featured in *Consequence Forum, Everyday Fiction, The Opiate, Pure Slush: Marriage, Pure Slush: Home*, and other magazines and journals.

Ellen Graham's (contributor) writing focuses on the West and stories of open spaces, both on the land and in the heart. Her work has been published in *Narrative, High Desert Journal, Everyday Fiction, Concrete Desert Review*, and *On the Run*. She is currently working on a series of stories about growing up in Salt Lake City.

Author of two award-winning books, **Susan E. Greisen** (contributor) finds stories and poems from her backyard to the rainforests of Africa and beyond. Her adventurous work and travel to more than fifty countries fuels her writing. Susan's intriguing website blog has readers from across the world (susangreisen.com).

Tyson Higel (contributor) lives in Bellingham, where he works as a nurse. He began writing poetry in search of fluent self-expression, something he struggles with as a person who stutters. His chapbook, *Confessions of a Stutterer* (Finishing Line Press, 2024), is available now.

Laura Kalpakian (editor) is the author of some seventeen novels published internationally and most recently, *The Great Pretenders* (2019). She is also the author of *Memory Into Memoir: A Handbook for Writers* (2021 University of New Mexico Press).

Shoshana D. Kerewsky (contributor) is a retired educator and psychotherapist. Her work has appeared in *fiction international, Crab Creek Review, Little Patuxent Review, Northeast Journal, HamLit,* and elsewhere. Her memoir, *Cancer, Kintsugi, Camino,* received a Firebird Award. Her latest book is *50 Days in May: Reflections Along the Camino de Santiago.*

Linda Lambert (contributor & editor) uses the surname Quinby to honor the adoptive parents who gave her free reign and free pedals to bike to the library. Libraries offered education (reading), employment (as a student and a late-in-life librarian), and, eventually, a wife (Amory). Both attended the 1991 White House Conference on Libraries.

In 2021 **Pat Matthews** (contributor) retired and moved from the Desert Southwest to the Kitsap Peninsula in Northwest

Washington. An excerpt from Pat's memoir, "Stardust" was recently published in, *True Stories* volume VII. She is writing a crime fiction novel and has happily begun writing poetry again.

Kenneth Meyer (contributor) and his wife, May, residents of Washington since 2013, spent most of their adult lives working overseas, primarily in China and the Middle East. Ken has a particular interest in non-Western cultures and ancient history. May is patient. Daughter Alanna is an officer in the Air Force.

John Miller (contributor) was born and raised in Coplay, a small town buried deep in the heart of Eastern Pennsylvania's Cement Belt. A former Peace Corps Volunteer to Liberia, John is a retired college professor living in Athens, Ohio, where he continues to teach and advise international students attending Ohio University.

Cynthia Mitchell (contributor) is a not-so-retired energy economist who is engaged in a variety of utility and climate-related issues. She draws on five decades of fighting climate change to write about the science and emotion of our environmental catastrophe.

Linda Morrow (contributor) is a native New Englander and a relative newcomer to the Pacific Northwest. Her memoir, *Heart of This Family: Lessons in Down Syndrome and Love*, is available wherever books are sold. She enjoys walking on deserted beaches, drinking coffee with friends, and spending time with family, including her two grandchildren.

Joe Nolting (editor) lives in Bellingham with his *esposa*, Cathy. He enjoys writing poetry, essays, and supporting humanitarian projects in Guatemala and El Salvador.

Martha (Patty) Oliver-Smith (contributor) is the author of a memoir, *Martha's Mandala*. She lives in Albany, Vermont, where she recently completed a second memoir, *Marnie's Voices*.

Beverly Ott (contributor) has felt a deep connection with the tiny worlds within our ecosystem since she was a child. She lives in Bellingham with her husband and dogs, with the forest as her backyard and the wild, rolling hills of Whatcom County as her playground.

Amory Peck (contributor) has been cancer-free since 1978. As a retiree, she identifies as a ponderer. She is most happy when reflecting, reading, and writing. Her favorite go-to spot on sunny days is a bench at Zuanich Park. On rainy days she's often tucked away in one of our Whatcom County libraries.

C.J. Prince (contributor), poet and artist, reads poetry across borders and writes handmade peace postcard poems to fly around the globe. Her work has been published in many anthologies. Prince received the Distinguished Poet medal from Writers International Network, Vancouver, British Columbia. Her newest poetry, *Pandamndemic: Poems in Isolation*, will be published after she fixes her roof.

Holly Redell-Witte (contributor) has been writing for newspapers and magazines for a long time, first in New York City, where she grew up, and now in Bellingham, Washington. Two years ago, at the Yale Writers' Workshop, she started down a different, more personal storytelling path. Writing, for her, is like drinking an elixir.

Ron Ruthruff (contributor) is an activist, author, and educator providing training and support for grassroots urban leaders in hard places around the world. His education is an eclectic blend of social work, counseling, and theological studies. He is the author of *The Least of These* and *Closer to the Edge*. He and his wife, Linda, live in south Seattle in the Rainier Valley, a multicultural neighborhood in the city.

Taya Sanderson Kesslau (contributor) has been a homeschool mother and CFO of a music business. She has worked at an animal shelter and practices as a Reiki Master. Her published work of poetry is titled *Seven Year Silence*. She lives in Fairhaven with her new husband and their many four-legged creatures.

Betty Scott's (contributor) Pacific Northwest poems, essays, and stories seek to embody the ever-present reality of rain's freedom-loving songs. She is grateful to walk in the woods, a place of unsubdued seasonal beauty. She enjoys Bellingham and Whatcom County productions, where fine music, art, literature, food, and friends reside and thrive.

Judith Shantz (contributor) is an aspiring writer living in Bellingham, Washington, who mostly writes fiction. In recent years, she has been encouraged to try other genres and has had memoir and poetry published in two Red Wheelbarrow Writers anthologies, *So Much Depends Upon . . .* and *This Uncommon Solitude*.

In another life, **Jes Hart Stone** (contributor) was an avid blue-water mariner. Her books on sailing are staples in the boating community. Today, she and her pup explore the forests of the Pacific Northwest and the mountains and beaches of Mexico. Stone writes non-fiction travel books and psychological thrillers.

Jean Waight (editor) writes memoir with a sociological bent, often exploring the tension between the individual and social belonging. She is the author of *The River Beyond the Dam: Shooting the Rapids of Progressive Christianity* and the forthcoming *In*

Timberline's Embrace: What an Old Lodge Taught Me About What's Worth Keeping.

Bob Warren (contributor) earned his master's degree in special education at Seattle University. His years of teaching students with special needs often inspire his thoughtful storytelling. Now retired, Bob lives with his wife in Kirkland, Washington, where he enjoys writing, local theater, the mountains, and sometimes even the famous rain.

Brenda Wilbee (contributor & editor) holds a master's degree in professional writing and is the author of ten books. Her work appears in several anthologies, including, no joke, a devotional Bible. When not writing, she directs the Tinnsy Winnsy Studio, a one-stop shop for writers looking to self-publish, offering editing, typesetting, and book design.

Acknowledgments

Red Wheelbarrow Writers . . . you are the creative spirits who come together monthly to share stories, to support and encourage each other, whether novice or seasoned author, and to collaborate on projects such as this, our fifth anthology. In the words of William Carlos Williams' poem from which we take our name, "so much depends upon" . . . the community of writers who make this book possible.

An enormous thank you to the members who went above and beyond to see this project through, especially Laura Kalpakian, a member of the selection committee, an editor, and Red Wheelbarrow Writers' founding mother with Cami Ostman and Susan Tive.

Jean Waight, Linda Lambert, Marian Exall, Seán Dwyer, Victoria Doerper, Joe Nolting, Randy Dills, and Susan Chase-Foster served on the selection committee and as editors to help writers polish their work for publication. Brenda Wilbee also served as an editor.

Huge gratitude to Lisa Dailey, our publisher at Sidekick Press, and to Andrea Gabriel for cover design.

Thanks also to the many locations that have housed our monthly Happy Hour meetings, most recently facilitated by

Michael and Dick Little. The wonderful team at Village Books and Paper Dreams continues to support writing in this community and is deeply appreciated.

www.ingramcontent.com/pod-product-compliance
Lightning Source LLC
Chambersburg PA
CBHW061736120626
46550CB00005B/1810